Fables in the Indian Narrative Tradition

An Analytical Study

Fables in the Indian Narrative Tradition

An Analytical Study

Dhananjay Singh

D.K. Printworld (P) Ltd.
Publishers of Indian Traditions

Cataloging in Publication Data — DK
[Courtesy: D.K. Agencies (P) Ltd. <docinfo@dkagencies.com>]

Singh, Dhananjay, 1975-

Fables in the Indian narrative tradition : an analytical study / Dhananjay Singh.

p. cm.

Originally presented as the author's thesis (Ph. D.) — Jawaharlal Nehru University.

Includes bibliographical references (p.) and index.

ISBN 13: 9788124605820

1. Fables, Indic — History and criticism. 2. Didactic literature, Sanskrit — History and criticism. I. Title.

DDC 398.20934 22

First published in India, 2011
ISBN 13: 978-81-246-0582-0 (HB) ISBN 10: 81-246-0582-3

Published and printed by:
D.K. Printworld (P) Ltd.
Regd. Office: 'Vedaśrī', F-395, Sudarshan Park
Ramesh Nagar Metro Station
New Delhi – 110 015
Phones : (011) 2545 3975; 2546 6019; *Fax* : (011) 2546 5926
E-mail: indology@dkprintworld.com
Web: www.dkprintworld.com

Preface

THE fable is the most metaphorical of all narrative genres. Its conception is governed by the compulsive need to establish a point or to make forceful a line of thinking. The Indian fable is a wonderful integration of the aesthetic and the discursive. It is both other-worldly and realistic. It is ideological. The Indian fable represents a major stream in the Indian narrative tradition. It imitates the social, political, religious, and moral systems of ancient India. It imitates the habits and chores, beliefs and realities of the Indian culture. While it is the dominant form in texts like the *Pañcatantra*, its inclusion at different places in the non-fable long narratives like the *Mahābhārata* and the *Yogavāsiṣṭha* is no less significant. In texts like the Jātakas, the fables occupy greater space than the non-fable narratives.

Each fable is a world in itself. The textual history of the *Pañcatantra* is itself no less interesting a narrative. Each fable has a history of conceptualisation and growth. But subsequent to their first enunciation, they become absorbed in the folk, because oral transmission has been the primary mode of narrative performance in India. Once they become part of the folk repertoire, the narratives share a common textual space; there are intertextual connections. A narrative like the one about the Monkey and Crocodile is found in the Jātakas as well as the *Pañcatantra*. But this does not mean they are the same. Each narrative is determined by the overall discursive system of the composition it is part of. For example, once the

Jātaka fable enters the narrative space of the *Pañcatantra*, its discursivity changes immensely. Not only its discussivity but also its form undergoes a major alteration.

The *Pañcatantra* is governed by the discourses enumerated in *Nāṭyaśāstra*. The Jātaka, on the other hand, foregrounds the religious and ethical agenda that originates from the Buddhist idea/ideal of the *bodhisattva*. The *Mahābhārata*, especially the small narratives, posits a political philosophy. Therefore, the fables contained in these compositions endorse the dominant ideology of the composition as a whole.

Indeed, the fables form a unique tradition. From the Jātakas to the modern folk tale, from about 300 BCE to contemporary India, the texts continue to be shared, however not without the changes brought in by the social and cultural life of the specific times. The form has been exploited as a major narrative mode of knowledge dispersion. Evidently, 300 BCE was the time when the fable had become very popular in India. The inscriptions on the reliefs of Bhārhut speak for the wide popularity of the Jātaka fables. It was around this time that fables from the Jātaka started to influence other fables like those in the *Pañcatantra*. From the Jātaka to the *Pañcatantra* and *Mahābhārata*, and from *Hitopadeśa* to the regional folk tales of India, the tradition still thrives.

The present work was originally submitted for the award of the degree of doctor of philosophy to the Centre for English Studies, Jawaharlal Nehru University, New Delhi, under the supervision of Professor Kapil Kapoor and Professor Santosh K. Sareen. It attempts a theoretical understanding and critical analysis of the various aspects of the classical Indian fable. The objective is to develop a conceptual frame for the Indian fables spread across various compositions. The narratives have been thoroughly studied in the context of their dominant discourses, their form and structure, and their continuing relevance seen in terms of the contemporary theory of narrative and discourse.

The work develops an overall understanding of the Indian fables, their genesis, their philosophy, their mutual relationships, their proliferation, their textual scholarship, and the like. There is an attempt made to establish the chronological development of the fable, right from the earliest fabular utterances found in the Vedas. Though the *Mahābhārata*, as far as the epic proper is concerned, precedes all the other fable-compositions, the fables themselves were a later inclusion in the epic. And hence, in the study, the Jātaka is discussed as the composition, which perhaps gave birth to the idea of the fully developed fable in India. The concept of the *bodhisattva* and the *buddhatva* is central to the understanding of the genesis of the Jātaka fables.

The *Mahābhārata* fables were inserted in the epic along with the other small narratives, legends, and folk tales. In the course of years of narration, the various narrators like the Sūtas and the Bhṛgus interpolated the fables along with the numerous other forms of small narratives in the text. However, these narratives have been perfectly placed in the text. Where Bhīṣma or Vidura or Śalya narrates a fable to Yudhiṣṭhira or Karṇa, the greater framework of the epic narrative achieves enhancement of meaning.

Indologists like Theodor Benfey, Johannes Hertel, Franklin Edgerton and Ludwik Sternbach have established through their scholarship of the *Pañcatantra* what great influence this work has had globally. From the earliest versions of this work, the Persian version and the *Tantrākhyāyikā* to the English and French adaptations, the fables of the *Pañcatantra* have been found everywhere. The history of the *Pañcatantra* reveals important facts about how a popular text might grow over a period of time. The *Hitopadeśa* is a major recension of the

Pañcatantra. Nārāyaṇa has not made a blind imitation of the source text, but in his recension is revealed how a text grows cumulatively in the Indian tradition. This is one reason why a text can never become obscure in India; because of its flexibility it remains relevant to each new period.

The most important preoccupation of the study is to analyse the Indian fable as a discourse. The fable-compositions give a clear impression in the beginning itself that they are conceived to serve larger ends. In fact, the narrative is made subservient to its discursive function. The Buddha narrates the fables to put across a particular religious discourse. The *bodhisattva* represents Buddhist principles like Compassion, Truth, Non-attachment and the like, and on each occasion the fable is committed to endorsing a particular Buddhist ideology. There are discursive passages in the text that are directed at the listeners with a serious intent. The genesis of each fable is determined by the effort of the Buddha to solve a particular problem, a specific ethical question, and throughout its narrativity, the fable is focused on it. The Jātakas, therefore, reveal a connection between ethics and narrative.

The discursive importance of the *Pañcatantra* is equally stressed. The text is, as it were, a compilation of the major texts of the Indian intellectual tradition. Numerous references to the authoritative texts of the different disciplines, *Arthaśāstra*, *Nāṭyaśāstra*, Dharmaśāstras, Āraṇyakas, Upaniṣads, the *Mahābhārata*, foreground the discursive foundations of the Indian fable. It is amusing to find the Crow quote from *Arthaśāstra*, or the Donkey give a lecture on *bhāva*s or the Cat talk about Dharmaśāstras, but behind the façade of fiction, the discursive texture of the fable is elaborate.

The *Pañcatantra* reveals the different political, legal, and social systems of ancient India, as enumerated in the knowledge texts. It presents situations that validate its dominant discourse of *nīti*, which is radically opposed to the religious discourse of tolerance, compassion, welfare of all beings, truthfulness and the like found in the Jātakas. The *Mahābhārata* also puts forth a distinct political ideology. The fable of Crow and Swan narrated by Śalya or the Jackal and the Tiger narrated by Bhīṣma is committed to endorsing a political thinking. The relationship between the king/state and the subjects is a major issue explored both in the *Pañcatantra* and the *Mahābhārata*.

The ideologies of the Indian fables get expressed through a wonderful sense of form that the narratives adopt. The fable has attained global popularity not only for its content but also for the relationship that exists between the form and the content. The fables are mostly set within a frame-narrative. The frame-narrative, as invented in the Indian fables, became so popular that the writers throughout the world have used it for different narrative genres. The relationship between the frame-narrative and the kernel narrative is explored in this study. The fables grow with a great sense of co-ordination between the narrative units and the discursive units. The story as a narrative and a discourse is discussed with special reference to the *Pañcatantra*, the Jātakas and the *Mahābhārata*. Another formal device invented by the Indian narrative tradition is *campū*, the mixing of the prose and verse within a single narrative. The Jātakas and the *Pañcatantra* make the best possible use of *gāthā*s (verses) in terms of the relations between the narrator and the reader. In *gāthā*s, the Buddha speaks directly to his listeners; the fictionality of the narrative is abandoned for that moment in the story when *gāthā* is uttered.

The study brings the Indian fables close to the conceptual frameworks found in the contemporary theory. This exercise is only to explore alternative models of analysis. There is no attempt to say that it is essential to speak of Indian literature in the context of the Western literary theory. However, the Indian fables do encourage a meaningful discussion of such theoretical issues as the author, the text, the story and the narrative, and the like.

This study would not have been possible without the inspiration, instruction, and benevolence of my *guru* Professor Kapil Kapoor. I will always remain grateful to "sir" for introducing me to Indian aesthetics and Indian literature. I am humbled by his greatness as a teacher and as a human being. I also owe immensely to Professor Santosh K. Sareen for his guidance and support as a supervisor.

I would like to express my acknowledgement to JNU Library, Sahitya Akademi, New Delhi, and Indira Gandhi National Centre for Arts, New Delhi, for providing the materials needed for my research.

I also owe this work to the support and guidance of my teachers and colleagues at the Centre for English Studies, JNU, Professors Makrand Paranjape, G.J.V. Prasad, Dr Saugata Bhaduri, and Dr Navneet Sethi.

To Seema, my wife, and our daughter, I owe all happiness that made this work possible.

I wish to express my gratitude to my uncle and aunt, my parents, my brother and sisters, friends, and all my teachers for all that they have done.

Finally, I would like to pay my respect to Shri Susheel Mittal and his D.K. Printworld, New Delhi, for accepting to publish this work.

Dhananjay Singh

Contents

Introduction

EVER since the first story-telling impulse in Vedas, the narrative as literary form and social practice has best described the various cultures and traditions of India. As a part of the oral tradition, the narrative developed amidst the Indian people more as performance. Both the stories as well as the occasion of story-telling brought the people together, and so it does now. Different stories are meant for different occasions. Each story was originally performed and received in the oral form, and so, even when they were later written down, like the Jātakas, the relationship between the story, the narrator and the audience, and the occasion of narration has remained an important principle in the organisation of the tales. From the mini narratives in the dialogue-form found in Vedas, and the stories in the Upaniṣads, the Itihāsas, and the Purāṇas, Kālidāsa's *mahākāvyas* (court epics), the *Yogavāsiṣṭha,* to the fables of the Jātakas, the *Pañcatantra* (and its various recensions, including the *Hitopadeśa*), the *Bṛhatkathā*, and the *Kathāsaritsāgara*, the Indian narrative tradition shows a remarkable diversity of form and content, and historico-cultural significance. The Indian narrative has in fact progressed in tandem with the progress of the communities and cultures of India, and vice versa.

Before going to discuss the Indian fable-narratives, which is the subject matter of this work, it would be appropriate to historically trace the development of the Indian narrative traditions, both in terms of form and content. As far as the form of the narratives is concerned, the Indian theorists like Bhāmaha (sixth century CE), Bhoja (eleventh century CE) and Viśvanātha Kavirāja (fourteenth century CE) have defined the various genres of narrative, along with the sub-categories of each genre that might help us to describe the genre of the fable.

> However, the long, continuous tradition of literary theory has led to a profusion of terminology, and this creates the interpretive problem of defining each term unambiguously to distinguish it from others. — Kapoor, 1996: 89

Broadly speaking, the Indian theoreticians have described three genres of narrative: (a) *kathā*, (b) *ākhyāyikā*, and (c) *ākhyāna*, which together make up *ākhyāna-jāti*, or a "class of narratives" (Kapoor, 1996: 89). The first conceptual term, *kathā*, encapsulates a thoroughly imagined narrative (*prabandha-kalpanā*), either in prose or verse, and is limited in its length and reach. *Ākhyāyikā* is a narrative in prose, and uses, for its content, materials from the tradition or history, and it could either be narrated in the first person, or let a narrator relate someone else's story. *Ākhyāna* is a narrative based on legends or myths, for example, the narratives in Vedas that form the context of the hymns, like the narrative of Yama and Yamī, Agastya and Lopamudrā, and Jābāli Satyakāma. The *Rāmāyaṇa* is classed as an *ākhyāna*, based as it is on the legendary lore of Rāma as the scion of the Raghu race.

As evident, *kathā* and *ākhyāyikā* are different on two accounts: (a) the former is a work of fiction, while the latter is based on history, and (b) the former could be either in verse or prose, whereas the latter is a prose narrative. Though Daṇḍin contends there exists no difference between the two forms of the Indian narrative, Bhāmaha points out a few more differences apart from the above two. Bhāmaha says that in *ākhyāyikā*, the hero has to give the accounts of his own deeds, whereas in *kathā*, the narrative should not be narrated by the hero himself but by someone else (De, 1924: 508).

Going by all these theoretical enumerations, the Indian fables could be categorised as *kathā*, but since they are closely connected to the history and the prevalent discourses of the times, they also share elements of *ākhyāyikā*. This much for the formal categorisation of the Indian fables.

Equally important it is to see the Indian fable-narratives historically develop over centuries in terms of their content. Now, the presence of rich and ever-evolving narrative traditions in India can be ascribed to the ontological status of *kathāvācana* (story-telling) in our culture. The story, as a ritualistic performance, has always had an existence characterised by its symbiotic relationship with its narrators-performers and the world it represents. Such a relationship between the narrative and the elements outside it comes directly from the relationship that existed between the human mind and the language, in the Indian tradition. Language itself came to the ancient Indian mind as story. *Vāc* or *śabda* is no empty mould for the meaning but, meaning itself that came in the narrative form. *Taittirīya Brāhmaṇa* states,

> All the Gods, the celestial spirits, men and animals live in the Word. In the Word all the worlds find their support.
>
> — Quoted in Panikkar, 2001: II.8.8.4

The Indian narrative tradition reveals a close relationship established in the Indian mind between the word and the world — the word as encompassing the divine and the human world. *Brahman* (the ultimate reality itself is the "Word", *śabda*), and then it is the "Word" that encompasses our being, our world, and our consciousness: "I will deliver this Word so that she will produce and bring into being this entire world" (quoted in Panikkar, 2001: II.8.8.4). It is this relationship between the word and the world that subsequently shaped the relationship between the narrative and the event. It is in the narrative and through it that we constitute our relationship with our families, our societies, our consciousness, and our histories. Like *Śabdabrahma* (the eternal Word-principle), the narrative is seen as the self-contained structure that can relate to and explicate the world at large, as is evident in Brāhmaṇas. Much before Roland Barthes, in his *Introduction to the Structural Analysis of Narratives,* deconstructed the subject-centred narrative of the West, making it a ubiquitous domain that constitutes all knowledge, the encrypted narrative in Brāhmaṇa texts had evolved, not authored by god or any human agency but as primordial enunciations: the Vedic narratives are *apauruṣeya* — the unauthored knowledge, indeed, primordial mystery comprising in herself the three worlds of time: past, present, and future. The Vedic narratives themselves constitute important theoretical statements, as is the case later with stories in the *Pañcatantra* and the *Hitopadeśa.*

The orally transmitted Vedas are apparently hymns, lyrical in form and devotional in content, but there are many hymns that interiorise the narrative structuration, as the story of friendship and enmity between Varuṇa and Vasiṣṭha in the *Ṛgveda,* 7.88. The sequence of the slyly suggested events and the use of dialogue contain the seed for the fuller development of a more elaborate narrative art in later times. There are wonderful little narratives embedded in the *Ṛgveda,* for instance, in the accounts of Yama and Yamī, Agastya and Lopāmudrā, Urvaśī and Purūravas, etc. In the subsequent ages of the Indian literary history, many of these little narratives have been reworked into extended forms in the Upaniṣads and the Āraṇyakas and even in the court literature and the plays of Kālidāsa.

The "Arthavāda" section of Brāhmaṇas explicates the rituals and various rules of conduct by suggesting forms which seem to pre-empt the various literary genres that developed later like Itihāsa, Purāṇa, *kathā,* etc. This narrative form stands out for its compact structure, with rarely any additional vocabulary. One reason for this compactness of form could be its formulaic nature. The contents of the ritualistic message had to be expressed orally, and so the formulas served as an aid to memory. In other words, Brāhmaṇas successfully systematised the modes of narrative dissemination that later was to culminate into the aphoristic form of *sūtra,* in which a mass of details was compressed within a minimum words (Bhattacharya, 2005).

The gradual evolution of the Indian narrative down the ages has never been bereft of the corresponding developments in the Indian philosophy. *Kathāvācana* has been a common mode, still popular in the Indian society, for the persuasive teaching of both the individual and the community as a whole. The Indian-ness of the narrative lies in its discursive dimension. Its literary scope encapsulates the epistemological function. Ever since the Ṛgvedic times, narrative has evolved as the most viable mode of knowledge dispersion. The Vedic hymns, the Upaniṣads, the Brāhmaṇas, and the Āraṇyakas have given a serious educative function to the mythic narrative. The word "myth" in the context of early Indian narratives does not signify an unreal imagining of past, but operates well within the scope of the real:

> In India a fabular mode of consciousness is inseparable from the epistemological mode. The mythic narrative is, therefore, used to disseminate knowledge. The mythic is different from the mythical since it is a disseminative mode, while the latter has a connotative association of non-real.
>
> — Bhattacharya, 2005

So, the narrative is not circumscribed within the aesthetic domain; the narrative, on the other hand, utilises strategies to promote *puruṣārthas* — the four ends of life: *dharma* (righteousness), *artha* (wealth), *kāma* (love), and *mokṣa* (liberation from here and now). "The merit of a literary composition is determined in a significant way by which of the four ends of life it promotes" (Kapoor, 2005). For the purpose of knowledge-dissemination, the narrative negotiates between philosophy and the community. The story is viewed as an autonomous and legitimate mode of thinking, a mode alternative to the intellectual and abstract theory making. The tales function both as primary knowledge statements and also as the illustrations of theoretical statements as is the case with the Upaniṣadic and the Buddhist narratives, as also with the *Pañcatantra*, the *Yogavāsiṣṭha*, and the Jātakas. Therefore, Indian poeticians stress upon the relevance of philosophy to literature, and make it important for the writers to be well-versed both in *loka* (world) and *śāstra* (knowledge-texts). The narratives are composed so that "the meanings of the knowledge-texts (Vedas) can be expounded and their validity comprehended" (Kapoor, 2005).

In the study of the narrative as an epistemological mode in India, there are paradigm shifts to be seen at different stages of Indian history that ushered in new traditions of narrative, as for instance, the Pāli Buddhist narrative tradition (the Jātakas) as against the Upaniṣadic tradition:

> India's oral tradition lends itself to wide-ranging story-telling: the Upaniṣadic *ākhyānas*, the Pāli Buddhist narratives, the encyclopaedic *Mahābhārata*, with innumerable sub-narratives, the Purāṇas, the fables of *Pañcatantra* and its recension *Hitopadeśa*, the strung narratives of *Kathāsaritsāgara*, folk retellings of the legends and myths, the romantic and heroic narratives of the folk traditions in the dialects of Indian languages — it is a vast and vital treasure house of stories. — Kapoor, 2005

All these narratives mark major transitions in the history of the Indian thought. The attempt, in this research work, is to analyse the discursive roots and the sources of the Indian fable-narrative tradition, among other issues.

A narrative tradition must not be seen only in itself, but also a larger understanding has to develop, as to how an emergence of a narrative tradition in a period contributed to the overall tradition, and also how older narratives continued not only to influence the content and style of the next generation narratives, but were even circulated with modifications, that the distinctiveness of the culture and milieu produced.

India's narrative traditions offer diverse developments. For instance,

> . . . The line of narratives from the Upaniṣads to the epics shows a shift of concern from *jñāna* (knowledge) to *bhakti* (devotion). But somewhere along the line, the Pāli Buddhist narratives also foreground *karma* (action) which then becomes a part of the epic-ethics as well.

For instance, the Jātaka tales postulate a definite break in the relationship between philosophy and narrative and narrative and ethics. In the Jātakas, "it is the human concern for the other that is postulated and validated as practical philosophy" (Kapoor, 2005).

So, the Pāli Buddhist narratives, containing the experiences of the *bodhisattva,* trace an improvement in the various *mārgas*, or paths of living postulated by the Indian thinkers by positing *karma* as against *jñāna* and *bhakti*. The narratives prior to the appearance of the Jātakas make *mokṣa* as their goal. The Upaniṣadic stories, for instance, Satyakāma of *Chāndogya Upaniṣad* and Naciketas of *Kaṭhopaniṣad,* delineate *mokṣa* to be attained through *jñāna*. These aspects of Indian philosophy and thought that influenced the narrative performance came for radical overhauling later when the *bodhisattva* postulated not *jñāna* but *karma* as the path of life, not personal salvation (*mokṣa*) but *nirvāṇa* and the welfare of all (*lokasaṁgraha*) as the goal of life, and human reason, *atipraśna*, the real experiences of suffering as more important than the metaphysical intuitions.

The fables found later in the *Pañcatantra* and the *Hitopadeśa* contribute yet another important dimension to the rich Indian narrative tradition, where *nīti* (policy) evolves as the third important category influencing the thought, content and style of narration.

This study has for its subject matter the fables in the *Mahābhārata* and *Yogavāsiṣṭha*, and complete fable-compositions like the Jātakas, the *Pañcatantra* and its various recensions including the most popular *Hitopadeśa*. One of the major interests of the study is to foreground the ideologies or the world views that these narratives promote. And hence, it was important to trace the philosophical background of these narratives, here. At the same time it must be admitted that it is difficult and not proper to make a sweeping remark about the philosophical bases of such comprehensive and profound texts like the *Mahābhārata*, because of the sheer diversity of the narratives found in them. However, it is assumed that the fables, in general, foreground discourses of a different nature. The narratives taken together make a distinct tradition within the vast gamut of the Indian literature:

> Unlike the other types of Indian poetical works, in this narrative literature the tendency is not to sketch only the stereotyped figures, but we meet here quite often several types of people — in fables men in the guise of animals — that exhibit a distinct physiognomy. And these men are

> barely virtuous kings or bold warriors, or beautiful princesses full of love, and venerable priests, as in the epic and mostly also in the drama too, but they are also people from other spheres of life. . . .
>
> — Winternitz, 1977: 332-33

The fable, as a distinct genre of narrative, has already been described as approximate to *kathā* and *ākhyāyikā*. It can be further said that it is a small narrative no longer than a short story, so structured as to point out a moral or a discourse. The discursive aspect of the fable is a major area of research covered by this study. The fable has also been a popular genre in the West since the early periods of the history there. The earliest preferment for the fable came from Plato himself who preferred a fabulist to Homer:

> Plato excluded Homer from his *Republic* and gave Aesop a place of honour, hoping that the young would absorb fables along with their mother's milk . . . since one cannot at too early an age acquire a love for wisdom and virtue.
>
> — Quoted in Mare, 1972: 30

There is a formidable lineage of fabulists in world literature that have been influenced by the Indian fables, like Aesop, Phaedrus, Hyginus, Jean de La Fontaine, Ivan Krylov and others. Interest in the fable cannot be dismissed as old and outdated as both the contents and forms of literature so written address some of the key questions facing the contemporary humanity. And again some of the most popular works like George Orwell's *Animal Farm* or Vikram Seth's *Frog and the Nightingale* show what great use a writer can make of the fable in different genres, which certainly shows greater adaptability of the fable-genre, in being fused into novel, poetry and drama alike. James Thurber's *Fables of Our Time* and Walt Disney's *Micky Mouse and His Friends* put to rest any doubt regarding the continuing relevance of the fable-narrative.

Not only the fables, but many other small narratives also originated in India, and then moved to other parts of the world, and became a part of human culture there:

> So far as my instructions go, I should be prepared, within certain limits, to hold a brief for India. So far as the children of Europe have their fairy stories in common, these — and they form more than a third of the whole — are derived from India. In particular, the majority of the Drolls or comic tales and jingles can be traced, without much difficulty, back to the Indian peninsula.
>
> — Jacobs, *Indian Fairy Tales*. http://www.sacred-texts.com/hin/ift/ift01.htm. Accessed on 7-3-2007

Even the movement of the Indian stories to the foreign shores has been an important area of research in the twentieth century. Researchers like Franklin Edgerton have studied especially how the Indian fables reached the different parts of the globe and got assimilated in the local literatures of the different countries.

In the first chapter of this study, the textual scholarship of the Indian fables, especially the *Pañcatantra*, has been analysed. It is extremely interesting to trace the origin and development of this text, which itself seems like a story. It is to the credit of the vast popularity of the Indian fables, that ironically the various Indologists had to reconstruct the lost text on the basis of its many versions. The Indian fables also reached different countries as individual stories. In other words, apart from the translations of the entire fable-compositions, in some cases individual fables were also taken to other countries. Some of the fables in Korea and Malaysia, for instance, originated in the *Pañcatantra*.

The textual history of other fable-compositions is equally interesting. In fact, the Jātakas would be the only composition of its kind in India that was put to writing as a deliberate policy, because after centuries of oral dissemination, it was thought the discursive elements in the texts might get lost or too corrupted. Since the Jātakas are also of religious importance — they are a part of the religious discourse of the Buddhists — it was thought that unless the narratives were put to writing, there might arise the risk of corruptions of the stories, and the teachings would not remain as they were narrated originally by the Buddha. So, in the various Buddhist Councils, the Jātakas were eventually committed to writing. However, the narratives were still very much a part of the oral tradition; they were integral to the folk imagination. The textuality of the *Mahābhārata* is also significant, as it reflects the oral traditions of India. It is interesting to note that the *Mahābhārata* fables are a much later inclusion, and therefore suggest how the epic continued to grow for a very long time.

However, it is just one of the many issues explored in the first chapter. One of the major interests of this chapter is to establish through the analysis of the various fable-compositions a sense of a tradition, ranging from the Jātakas to the *Hitopadeśa*. There are also discussions about how each composition has progressed over centuries of developments, and how the fables came to be a part of the larger texts like the *Mahābhārata*. Though all these compositions, the Jātakas, the *Mahābhārata*, the *Yogavāsiṣṭha*, the *Pañcatantra*, and the *Hitopadeśa* foreground their own philosophies and their own discourses, there are linkages to be established as well. For example, many of the fable-compositions share each other's stories. The frame-narrative of the third book of the *Pañcatantra*, about the war between the owls and the crows, comes from Aśvatthāmā's experience under a tree after the defeat of Duryodhana in the *Mahābhārata*. Again, the narrative about the pair of hospitable doves in the *Pañcatantra* is the same as the narrative in "Śānti-Parva" of the *Mahābhārata*.

Further, the remnants of the Lion and the Bull story of the *Pañcatantra* are to be found in the Jātaka No. 361.

Though they may share narratives, the ideologies proposed by the different fable-compositions are, however, generally very different. This is a unique thing about the Indian fable tradition. Though, even historically, most of the fables across these compositions proliferated almost simultaneously, during the same time, from about third century BCE onwards, they, in most cases, subject the narrative to the overall discourse of the respective composition. The Jātaka fables are based on the idea of the *bodhisattva* as discussed in the first chapter. The *Pañcatantra* fables again are meant for political instructions of the princess referred to in the same chapter.

Indeed, the fable as a discourse is a major preoccupation of this study, and is explored in more detail in the second chapter. The narratives not only suggest the contemporary social, political, and religious thought by way of themes and situations, but also cite directly from the knowledge-texts of the Indian tradition. The references contained in fables establish that the knowledge-texts like the *Arthaśāstra,* the *Nāṭyaśāstra,* the *Nītiśāstra,* the *Mahābhārata,* the *Mahābhāṣya,* the Dharmaśāstras, the Mīmāṁsāsūtras were part of the folk wisdom, and therefore, the characters in the fables quote freely from these texts, and discuss the issues contained in them.

Through the fables, a reader can establish not only the systems that governed the life in the courts, but also the life of the common people. In the *Pañcatantra,* there are references to community living, to legal disputes, and the manner in which they were sorted out, as in the fable of the cunning Cat; there are references to the various principles of practical living. The fables also foreground the duties of the king and the state, the strategies adopted during war times, the relationship between the king and his subjects, among many other issues. In general, the discourses in the *Pañcatantra* are oriented towards *nīti* (polity), which is political in its implication, and amounts to attaining benefits and success through intelligent means.

The *Mahābhārata* fables are again, as is obvious from the general nature of the epic, replete with various kinds of knowledge. But the dominant discourse is the political discourse. The fable of the Crow and the Swan in "Karṇa-Parva," and the Jackal and the Tiger in "Śānti-Parva," for instance, enumerate important political strategies and principles.

The fable, therefore, is not about anything, it is that thing itself. The fable is the discourse. The Jātakas reveal an entirely different purpose with the fable. The same fables, whereas in the *Pañcatantra* iterate the ways that would bring comfort to the self, in the Jātakas, they foreground the *dhamma* professed by the *bodhisattva*. Each fable is based on one of the 10 Buddhist principles. What is most noteworthy about the fables here is the ethical ambience that the telling of the tale creates.

If these fables deliberately push a political or religious agenda, they also make upfront their connection with the folk. It is really interesting to see that many of the fables contained in these compositions gradually became part of the regional Indian folk. It is equally a novel experience to note the similarities and differences in the folk tales that freely adopted from the fable-compositions. The second chapter discusses this issue with a few examples.

The Indian fables, if they communicate distinct ideologies, also demonstrate an uncanny use of the formalistic device of arranging the narratives. World literature got the device of frame-narratives from the Indian fable-compositions. It is remarkable how the *Pañcatantra* manages to interweave a meandering series of narratives together with a perefect use of the framing device. Related with this is the connection between time, narrative, and discourse in the Indian fables. Along with the issue of frame-narrative, the relationship between time and narrative, narrative and discourse, and the device of mixing prose with verse (*campū*) are discussed in the third chapter.

Time as a factor is very important in the integration of narrative units, especially in the Jātaka fables. It is because the narratives make a progress across time. The shift from the present to the past and back to the present leads to a development of the notion of universal time, and the process of narrativity has to be discussed in this context. The relationship between narrative and discourse is again a marked feature underlying the Jātaka fables, as also the other fable compositions. In fact, each story can be classified into narrative and discursive texts, as discussed in this chapter.

Campū, as a narrative device, is again the contribution of the Indian fables to the world literature, as writers still today continue to use verse at appropriate places in the prose narrative to serve various purposes. In the Indian fables, the verse is used not to heighten the emotions but as a discursive strategy by the narrators. The verse appearing in the narrative contains the entire intent of the story.

The fourth and last chapter attempts a more contemporary reading of the fables. It is important to analyse the fables in the light of recent Western literary theory. To discuss how the narratives are amenable to newer interpretations seemed an effort worth taking. The narratives are discussed in terms of the postmodernist and post-structuralist concepts of the author and the text, Bakhtin's distinction between prose and poetry, and his "dialogism," and some of the issues taken up by the structuralist narrative poetics.

More special is the discussion of the issue of the authorship, which is also hinted by way of a passing remark at the end of chapter one. In the Indian tradition, authorship has never been an issue to deliberate over. Author is simply a function in the Indian tradition, in the same way as Foucault calls him/her a function, a name to identify the texts. There is no issue in the narratives to identify the voice of the author. The narratives are in fact individual distinct systems, and the fact that the texts were a part of the oral tradition makes them more distant from any authorship.

1

Fables in India
An Overview

> The invention of the fable is the most enviable exertion of human genius: it is the discovering of a truth to which there is no clue, and which, when once found out, can never be forgotten. — William Hazlitt (quoted in Blackham, 1985)

THE corpus of fables in India reveals a tradition, in the same way as other forms of Indian literature are defined best by their tradition. The Indian narrative tradition is not author-specific nor is it constrained by space and time; it is a cumulative tradition that makes it possible for a body of narrative literature to continuously enrich by new additions and omissions necessitated by the mutable contexts and requirements of each period of Indian history. And yet amidst the new developments one can still trace the old nucleus of a particular narrative tradition, the basic texts that the tradition, thriving on the oral communication of stories, keeps intact from one generation to the other. India has a distinct fable tradition. The various collections of fables in India exhibit a tradition, which can historically be roughly placed from 300 BCE to about CE 1400, a tradition from the Jātakas to the *Hitopadeśa*. But, for the primitive evidence of the fables in India we have to go still further back to Vedas. In the same way, the tradition still prospers in the folk narrations as well as the adaptations and redactions for school textbooks and animation movies.

It is now well established beyond doubt that the genesis of the fables rests with India. There did exist a view prior to the twentieth century that the Indian fables had been borrowed from Greece, and that they had originated from the fables of Aesop. But this could not stand the increasing evidence found during years of research on the Indian fables by the Western scholars since the latter half of the nineteenth century. The new findings clearly pointed to the fact that the Indian fables were either independent of the Greek or, more likely, were composed even before the Greek.

> In fact, now it is generally held that the parallelism between the *Aesop* and the Jātakas in a dozen or more beast fables is due to a transmission of folk tales from India to Greece via Persia and Asia Minor. — Jackson, 1918: 281

However, as we shall read in the subsequent chapters, it is not the antiquity alone that explains the Indian fable tradition. The fables in the various composed texts are marked for their surprisingly modern discursive content and aesthetics, their rich texture and form, the folk-traditions that they uphold, the narrative contexts that they explore, and their enviable universality that proverbs like "that's like the story of the fox and crow" spoken in a British or Chinese society are traced to the Indian fables (Blackburn, 1996: 496).

But to remain with the nucleus of the fable tradition in India for some time, we can attribute the early origin and popularity of the Indian fables to the popular Indian philosophy of an organic community that does not distinguish between Man/Woman and his/her animal-neighbour, which is not built on binaries like God/Man, Man/Animal, etc. The popular belief in India, since the early times, has been derived from the sense of coexistence of various beings. Therefore, attributing human virtues and vices to the animals was no surprise to the Indian mind.

> To invest inanimate objects as well as non-human creatures with the capacity to feel, think and speak probably stems from the animistic or atavistic beliefs of the early times.
>
> — Panikker, 2003: 12

So, the animal stories could be perfectly used both as aesthetic and discursive practice in India.

The earliest use of the fable form in the Indian narrative tradition dates as far back as to the *Ṛgveda*. The famous hymn in the *Ṛgveda* VII compares a group of brāhmaṇas with the croaking frogs as they chant while performing sacrifices. This contracted narrative makes it evident that the Indian mind from the earliest saw and understood that human meanings could be communicated by creating animal characters, and giving them human voice and attitudes. It was only proper that this should have led to the development of more elaborate fables later.

There are also many instances in *Chāndogya Upaniṣad* (I.12), where, for example, we come across the story of the dogs. A pack of dogs gathers around a white dog so that the latter would procure food for them through hymns. This particular narrative is a sort of prototype for fable-narrative with all the allegorical implications. In *Chāndogya Upaniṣad* (IV. 1; 5; 7; 8) again, there is the narrative about Jñānaśruti who attempts to draw the attention of Sage Raikva by way of the conversations between two flamingoes. The most popular of the Upaniṣadic narrative, with fable-like features, is that of Satyakāma, who gets instructions from a bull, a flamingo, and a swan on the trot. Though not as developed as modern fables, these narratives are a definite stage in the development of the fables in India. They make good representation of human motifs through animal characters.

The various statements contained in the knowledge-texts of the Indian tradition convey that the fables attained a much developed form and popularity among our people fairly early in the Indian history. The references in these texts substantiate that fabular narratives were widely shared in the Indian society by the second-century BCE Patañjali's *Mahābhāṣya*, a commentary on Pāṇini's *Aṣṭādhyāyī*, which is a major text in the Indian intellectual tradition. It seems Patañjali exploited the fable as tools for grammatical description and intellectual analysis. Expressions like *kākataliyam*, "unexpected, as in the fable of the crow that was killed by a palm-fruit falling down," and *ajakṛ, paṇiyam*, "in the manner of the she-goat and the dagger or in that of the she-goat killed by a dagger" appear in his composition (quoted in Winternitz, 1977: 336). Unless the fables were popular, the grammarian would not have felt the temptation to simplify the complex grammatical forms by employing analogies from the fables.

The widespread popularity of the fable and its suitability as a means of disseminating both intellectual ideas and folk-knowledge, in another instance, is suggested by the inclusion of many fables in the later compilations of the *Mahābhārata*. The *Mahābhārata* developed over centuries from its core story of the war, and the fact that fables were also one of the narrative forms included in it suggests that they did circulate as popular folklore at that stage of the Indian history. Critics are, however, divided whether the folklore borrowed fables from literature or the literary compositions adapted the fables from the folklore. In either case, the growing fondness for the fables in the Indian people is no doubt established.

The major compositions that altogether make the fable-tradition of India are the Jātakas, the *Mahābhārata*, the *Pañcatantra*, and its various recensions like the *Tantrākhyāyikā*, *Bṛhatkathāmañjarī*, *Kathāsaritsāgara* and the *Hitopadeśa*. It is extremely challenging to delineate a chronology, as difficult it is to categorise these compositions as one homogeneous body of fables, on the basis of their fabular content. To take the second issue first, there is a great deal of heterogeneity as each composition of fables has its own discursive purpose. Moreover, they were written in different periods of our history, and are, therefore, influenced by different knowledge systems.

The narratives found in each collection are specific to the overall design and intent of the work they are part of, notwithstanding the fact that some fables have been found in more than one composition. Whereas the Jātaka fables are narrated within the immediate context of the Buddhist religious discourse, the *Mahābhārata* and the *Pañcatantra* fables contain political treatises rendered in the narrative form. Some of the *Mahābhārata* fables also fall within the knowledge-systems of the Vedas. Hence, it is difficult to homogenise them. It is true that a Jātaka fable like the one about the Monkey and the Crocodile, in *Vānarinda-Jātaka* (No. 57), is also to be found in the *Pañcatantra*, but the intent of this same fable, once it becomes a part of another composition, takes a different colour influenced by the other fables found in that composition, say, the *Pañcatantra*.

Though there have been researchers and scholars of Indian literature like Ludwik Sternbach and Franklin Edgerton who have attempted genealogies of fable-compositions, as for instance, *Pañcatantra*, it is very difficult to construct a genealogy or chronology of the Indian fable-tradition as a whole. If at all we call this a tradition, it would be difficult to speak of the Indian fable as a linear tradition based on temporal order of one composition after the other. To a great extent, this tradition is characterised by a great deal of simultaneity of fable development, and even exchange. The biggest constraint in the way of constructing a chronology of Indian fable-tradition is that we lack unquestionable certainty about the dates of these compositions.

Apparently, the fables from the *Mahābhārata* seem the oldest, and therefore, most likely, deserve the first place in the tradition of Indian fables. E.W. Hopkins in his *The Great Epic of India: Character and Origin of the Mahabharata*, suggests that "the time of this epic poetry may lie as far back as 700 BCE or 1700 BCE" (Hopkins, 1993: 386). The proximity of the work with the pre-classical Upaniṣads and with Vedas, even more, consolidates its antiquity. As an Itihāsa, the work has enjoyed equanimity even with Vedas:

> *Chāndogya Upaniṣad* regards the Itihāsas and Purāṇas as the fifth Veda. This shows that alongside the Vedic literature, there also existed some collections of Itihāsas and Purāṇas, made up of myths and legends of gods, snake-deities, sages, warriors and kings of ancient times.
>
> — Verma, 1988: 11

Going by this account, we might consider the fables in the *Mahābhārata* as earliest among the fables in India, if we leave aside the seeds of the fable found in the *R̥gveda* and Upaniṣads. In fact, there is a school of critics which believes that the fables originated with the *Mahābhārata*. The German critic, Maurice Winternitz, upholds this line of thinking.

> In Indian literature, we come by the earliest actual fables in the *Mahābhārata*, and in fact, both in the epic proper and as also in book XII. — Winternitz, 1977: 335

But critical opinion is stronger in favour of the view that the fables in the *Mahābhārata* are later than the Jātaka fables. It is an accepted view generally that small narratives are a much later inclusion in the epic proper, and therefore, the Jātaka fables, which were fairly well known by the third century BCE, come in contention for being the oldest fables, and therefore the prototype of the fable in India. Edward Washburn Hopkins argues that it cannot

> be supposed that epic poetry was suddenly invented by one poet. The numerous "ancient tales" of epic character must have furnished a large body of epic phrase as well as fable, out of which and on the basis of which arose our present epic . . . the epic itself admits that the present work is not an original work. — Hopkins, 1993: 64-65

So, the *Mahābhārata* was not composed by a single author at any particular time, but in its present form, it grew and developed gradually over centuries with the addition of a great collection of most diverse literature that grew around the nucleus, the fable being one such literature. The great epic of India can be divided into two parts broadly: the core story of the Kauravas and the Pāṇḍavas, and the enormous tale-literature. "It appears to be a heterogeneous collection of strings wound about a nucleus almost lost sight of. The nucleus, however, is a story" (Hopkins, 1993: 363). According to Hopkins, the origin and the development of the *Mahābhārata* can be understood in four stages:

1. *400 BCE* — At this stage, what we have is a collection of the Bharata lays. In this, there is no reference to the Pāṇḍavas.
2. *400-200 BCE* — There is a major development at this stage. The Pāṇḍavas emerge as the heroes of the epic and Kṛṣṇa comes as the demi-god.
3. *300 BCE - CE 100/200* — Here, Kṛṣṇa becomes the all-powerful god. There are major interpolations of didactic literature. New episodes are added, and it is here that the fables enter the epic.
4. *CE 200-400* — At this stage, the introduction to the first book of epic (and the last books also) is added.

Hopkins opines that the didactic sections of the *Mahābhārata* including fables were included between 300 BCE and CE 100 or 200. His assertion has been accepted by most critics.

The didactic tales in the *Mahābhārata* are ascribed to the Sūtas and the Bhṛgus.

> There were professional story-tellers or Sūtas, Aitihāsikas and Paurāṇikas, who used to recite these tales . . . all these accounts gradually formed parts of the *Mahābhārata* which became the repository of the Indian thought and culture.
>
> — Verma, 1988: 11

The Sūtas included the ballads and the historical events in the "Jaya" and Bhṛgus put the religious and ethical sections in the *Mahābhārata.* The Sūtas didn't meddle with the popular records of the tradition and also kept intact the original form of folklore.

> Thus the Bhṛgus should be regarded as the authors and the narrators of these fables, being influenced by the device of Buddha and Viṣṇu Śarma, the author of the popular *Pañcatantra.* — Kawthekar, 1965: 127

The inclusion of fables in the *Mahābhārata* coincided with the origin and development of the *Pañcatantra,* and critics argue that both were inspired by the Buddhist Jātakas. It is believed that it was the Buddha who, for the first time, exploited the fable for the means of spreading knowledge by telling stories about his previous births as a monkey, a goat, a mouse, and so on and so forth. In this way, he found the most perfect method to inculcate a religious doctrine or moral in the minds and hearts of the people. The idea was really successful because subsequently the fable form became so popular that the fables had to be carved on the *stūpa*s of Bharhut in the third century BCE.

So, while discussing the fable tradition of India, barring aside the animal stories found in the *Ṛgveda* and Upaniṣads, we have to consider the Jātakas as the original of the form, and accept that the *Mahābhārata* fables and the *Pañcatantra* grew simultaneously modelled on the Buddhist fable. Theodor Benfey in his introduction to his translation of the *Pañcatantra* argues that the original *Pañcatantra* was a Buddhist treatise. He made this claim on the basis of a Buddhist extract that he found in the Syriac translation of the *Pañcatantra* made in about CE 570. This particular fable was also found later in a Tibetan work.

The point that comes out in a way is that the fable had become extremely popular around the third century BCE, and, henceforth, began flourishing simultaneously in the versions of Jātakas like the *Jātakamālā*, the *Mahābhārata* and the *Pañcatantra*. The fable of the Clever Fox, for instance, found in the *Pañcatantra* is also there in the *Mahābhārata*. The fable of the Goat and the weapon narrated aphoristically by Vidura in the *Mahābhārata* is also found in the *Takkarida Jātaka*.

T.W. Rhys Davids, who pioneered the modern Buddhist studies, claims in his *Buddhist Birth Stories* that the Jātaka fables were responsible for the genesis of many of the narratives in the West. The origin of the Jātakas lies in the doctrine of metempsychosis. The composition constitutes a voluminous collection of folklore and fables. They are a part of the Pāli canon of Theravāda Buddhism. The narratives are included in *Khuddaka Nikāya* of *Sutta Piṭaka*. *Sutta Piṭaka* is one of the three divisions of the *Tipiṭaka*, which is a Pāli canon. The other two parts of the *Tipiṭaka* are *Vinaya Piṭaka* and *Abhidhamma Piṭaka*. It is a collection of Buddhist writings and contains more than 10,000 *sutta*s (teachings) of Buddha or his close disciples. The Jātakas are also called one of the nine *aṅga*s or limbs of the Pāli canon. The other eight are (a) *sutta* (the teachings of the Buddha compiled in the prose form, (b) *geyya* (sermons in the mixed form of verse and prose, (c) *veyyākaraṇa* (expositions), (d) *gāthā* (stanzas), (e) *udāna* (utterances of wonderment), (f) *itivuttaker* (concise sayings), (g) *adbhuta dhamma* (description of supernatural power), and (h) *vedalla* (solution of problems in the format of questions and answers) (Banerjee, *Pali Literature*. http://www.ibiblio.org/radha/rdindex1.htm. Accessed on 10-11-2005).

It is difficult to determine the actual number of the Jātakas. According to *Niddesa*, a book of *Khuddaka Nikāya*, generally speaking, the total number of the Jātakas is 500. This fact is also endorsed by Fa-hian (Faxian), the famous Chinese traveller, who visited India and Abhayagiri in Sri Lanka as a Buddhist pilgrim. In his memoirs, he has recorded 500 representations of the *bodhisattva* in successive births. The *Sāketa-Jātaka* (No. 68) says that Śākyamuni Buddha had 1500 births. However, the Fausboll's edition, a standard modern collection of the Jātakas, contains 547 narratives.

The Jātakas are a unique collection of Indian fables as they are derived from the famous Buddhist lore about the many birth stories of the Buddha. In these birth stories the Buddha appears as the *bodhisattva* (one who has not yet attained *nirvāṇa*), in both animal and human form, in which he is born as a brāhmaṇa, a king, a merchant, a hare, a fish, etc. In each of these births, the Buddha, in the *bodhisattva* state demonstrates extraordinary qualities like compassion, self-denial, and magnanimity. In the study of the Jātaka fables, we are primarily interested in his *bodhisattva* experiences as the one born as an animal. As an animal character, the *bodhisattva* appears, among others, as an iguana in *Godh Jātaka*; a jackal in *Sigāla Jātaka*; a rooster in *Kukkuṭa Jātaka*; a crow in *Kāka Jātaka*; as an elephant in *Chaddanta* and *Silava Jātaka*; a fish in *Mitachinti Jātaka*; a buffalo in *Mahiṣa Jātaka*; a bull in *Nandivisāla* and *Sarambha Jātaka*; a frog in *Hāritimata Jātaka*; a *garuḍa* in *Sussondi Jātaka*; a goose in *Neru Jātaka*; a hare in *Sasa Jātaka*; a horse in *Ajanna* and *Bhogajanna Jātaka*; a wild duck in *Naccha Jātaka*; a woodpecker in *Javasakuna* and

Khadiravaniya Jātaka; a peacock in *Baveru* and *Mahāmora Jātaka*; a pig in *Mahātuṇḍila Jātaka*; a pigeon in *Kapota, Romaka, Lola, Kāka Jātaka*; a quail in *Vattaka* and *Sammodamana Jātaka*; a monkey in *Kapi, Mahākapi, Nalapana,* and *Suṁsumāra Jātaka*; a lion in *Gula* and *Sigāla Jātaka*; a parrot in *Potthapada, Pupphaka* and *Jambuka Jātaka*; a snake in *Champeyya, Saṅkhapala, Bhūridatta,* and *Mahabhaddara Jātaka*; a vulture in *Gijjha Jātaka*; and a cat in *Aggika* and *Bilāra Jātaka*.

The Jātaka fables reveal a comprehensive view of the quest of the *bodhisattva*, as he undergoes various stages of birth and rebirth, and the experiences contained in each birth, to become a Buddha. The concept of rebirth finds greater acceptance among the Indian people, who are used to the reconstruction of the previous lives of the saints and greater beings that belong to the sacred tradition. These stories are narrated by the Buddha after he has attained the *buddhatva*. The Buddha was committed to taking his religious teachings to the masses, but he well understood the importance of story-telling as a method. So grew an enormous material which has come down to posterity as the Jātakas, and influenced people worldwide. These same stories during their long history of wanderings came to be used by Boccacio or Poggio or Chaucer. Chaucer, for instance, has used the *Vedabdha Jātaka* in his *Canterbury Tales*. He unwittingly sets up a Jātaka story to be told by the Pardoner — his tale of "the ryotoures three".

Any study of the Jātaka fables requires that the concepts of the "Buddha" and the *bodhisattva* be properly understood. The "Buddha," though it is well known as Śākyamuni Gautama Buddha (543-483 BCE), is not a proper name; it is a generic and appellative name which means the one who has attained Enlightenment. Now, the protagonist of every Jātaka narrative, including the fables, is the *bodhisattva*. A *bodhisattva* is the one whose aspiration is to attain *bodhi* or Enlightenment. This being shows through his words and deeds that he has it in him to become the Buddha for the good and *mokṣa* (liberation) of all the beings that he comes across. In fact, he proclaims this wish with great resolve.

A *bodhisattva* sets himself on the quest of developing the unique qualifications of the Buddhahood (*buddhakārakadhamma*), and in the process seeks 10 perfections (*parami*), which are *dāna* (charity), *sīla* (right-conduct), *nekkhama* (dispassionateness), *panna* (wisdom), *viriya* (steadfastness), *khanti* (forbearance), *saccā* (truthfulness), *adhitthana* (pledge), *metta* (loving compassion), and *upekkhā* (non-attachment). In each of the various births of the *bodhisattva*, it is actually the struggle for these 10 perfections, which constitutes the subject matter of the Jātaka narrative. So, in other words each Jātaka fable is rather an exemplification of the *bodhisattva*'s struggle for *parami*/perfection. In addition to the *parami*, a *bodhisattva* should develop four *bhūmis*, which are, *ussaha* or *viriya* (zeal), *ummagga* or *panna* (wisdom), *avatthāna* or *adhitthāna* (resolution), and *hitachariya* or *metta* (compassion). Then, he practises six *ajjhasayas* or the factors essential to *bodhi*.

The Jātaka No. 35, for instance, is a validation of truthfulness. It is titled *Vattaka Jātaka*, and in this narrative the *bodhisattva* is born as a quail. In this narrative, the young quail (*bodhisattva*) demonstrates a tremendous wisdom and precocious knowledge about goodness and truth that surely signifies that he would become the Buddha. The forest in which he was lying in a nest is engulfed by a fire. All the birds and other inhabitants of the forest run away to safety, including his parents who forsake him at this dangerous hour. Naturally, the young quail pensively reflects:

Had I the power to put forth my wings and fly, I would

> wing my way hence to safety; or, if I could move my legs and walk, I could escape elsewhere afoot. Moreover, my parents, seized with the fear of death, have fled away to save themselves, leaving me here quite alone in the world. I am without protector or helper. What, then, shall I do this day?
>
> — *The Jātaka*, 1990: 89

The young quail's ability to reflect upon the issue at this hour of danger and crisis is only possible for the one who is truly blessed with great inner strength and universal knowledge. At such a time, when a common being would be beset by fear and anxiety, the young quail, Buddha-to-be dwells on an important Buddhist discourse on what it needs to be the Buddha, and how someone like the Buddha would deal with the situation that he confronts. He thinks:

> In this world there exist what is termed the Efficacy of Goodness, and what is termed the Efficacy of Truth. There are those who, through their having realised the Perfections in the past ages, have attained beneath the Bo-tree to be All-Enlightened; who, having won Release by goodness, tranquility and wisdom, possess also discernment of the knowledge of such Release; who are filled with truth, compassion, mercy, and patience; whose love embraces all creatures alike; whom men call omniscient Buddhas. . . . And I too grasp one truth . . . and by an Act of Truth to make the flames go back, to the saving both of myself and the rest of the birds.
>
> — *The Jātaka*, 1990: 90

At the end, the young quail expresses the secret of his escape from the all-threatening fire, in the form of a *gāthā*:

> I wrought my act of Truth, and therewithal
> The sheet of blazing fire left sixteen lengths
> Unscathed — like flames by water met and quenched.
>
> — *The Jātaka*, 1990: 90

In a similar vein, all the Jātaka fables delineate one of the perfections that the *bodhisattva* must attain so as to be considered as the one who might become a Buddha. The fables give an interesting form to the thoughts inherent in the perfections that the *bodhisattva* strives for, and the message becomes very popular among the people.

The Jātakas, as is true about any Indian cultural text, existed in the oral form as a living tradition. That is why it is very difficult to determine the actual length of the narratives, though they were put to writing later, because the Jātakas were meant to be told and not to be read. Therefore, it is difficult to estimate their length in terms of the written page. However, for the sake of making a point they are of varied lengths. While in the first three books, comprising about 300 Jātakas, only 11 stories are 6 to 10 pages long, about 260 are only 1 to 3 pages long, in the *Mahānipāta*, even the shortest Jātaka is of 11 pages and longest contain as many as 90 pages. For several centuries, the fables of the Buddha survived through its circulation among the folk by way of oral narration by the monks:

> It is quite uncertain when these various birth-stories were put together in a systematic form such as we find in our present Jātaka collection. At first they were probably handed down orally, but their growing popularity would ensure that their kernel, at any rate, would ere long be committed to some permanent form. — *The Jātaka*, 1990: xxii

Later, the need of committing them to writing was realised. In fact, the Jātakas, though they also offer a religious discourse, were never part of the Buddhist scriptures. Indeed, even the biography of the Buddha is not to be found in any scripture of the Buddhists, but later they were developed by the Buddhist schools. It is important here to put the Jātakas in the proper perspective of their development by establishing their place in the Buddhist/Pāli canon, by accounting for their collection in a proper form. At the same time, it is important to mention here that the Jātakas were extremely popular in their oral forms before they were compiled. Even before the first council met, Plato (429-347 BCE) refers to the story of the donkey donning a lion's skin and scaring away people, which originally belonged to one of the most popular Jātakas, known as the *Siṁhacamma Jātaka*.

The entire corpus of the Buddhist literature, which includes the Jātakas, was compiled during the four councils of monks convened at different times after the death (*mahāparinirvāṇa*) of the Buddha. The first council was called immediately after Buddha's *mahāparinirvāṇa* in the Saptāriṇī cave in Rājagṛha. This council was held under the chairmanship of Mahākassapathera. In all, 500 direct disciples of lord Buddha, including Upāli and Ānanda, were present in that council. All of them recited the teachings of the Buddha from their memory. It was in this council and through this recitation that *dhamma* (i.e. *sutta*, discourses) and *vinaya* (i.e. monastic rules) were codified. The compilations at this council are regarded as marking the beginning of the *Tipiṭaka*.

Hiuen Tsang said that 110 years after the death of the Buddha, the second council was convened at Valukarama in Vaiśālī. Seven hundred scholarly *bhikṣus* attended this council. This council was called to sort out some minor discrepancies in the interpretation of the monastic rules that had crept in, as almost anyone could interpret them. This council did not make any attempt to write down the teachings of the Buddha, but the idea to give a definite form to his teachings was discussed.

The third council of the Buddhist monks and scholars was called in the third century BCE, probably during the reign of Emperor Aśoka. The Buddhist canon faced a threat of schism by the different sects. To deal with this threat, Aśoka convened this council to give a final touch to the compilation of the *Tipiṭaka* in terms propounded by the Theravāda school that he himself belonged to. The Jātakas were a part of the canon professed by this school.

It was in the fourth council convened by King Vattagamani that the Pāli canon, mainly the Theravāda canon, including the Jātakas, was finally agreed upon and written down. It happened in the first century BCE. Until this council, the Pāli *Tipiṭaka* was handed down in oral form. Even when Mahindathera and Saṅghamitta, Aśoka's son and daughter, went on a mission to Sri Lanka, they had taken with them the *Tipiṭaka* in the oral form only.

So, we can already see that for the future of the Jātaka fables the fourth council was very crucial, though scholars believe that the narratives were given a final shape long after in the fifth century CE by Buddhaghoṣa. It was in this council that the Jātaka fables were entered into the *Suttapiṭaka,* in one of its *nikāya*s (divisions) — the *Khuddaka Nikāya*. It is the fifth *nikāya,* and it exists as a collection of the short pieces. Now, the tenth book of *Khuddaka Nikāya* is called the Jātaka, which comprises 6653 *gāthā*s (verses) and 547 Jātakas, the fables.

However, the Jātakas are not only confined to the *Sutta Piṭaka*. The oldest examples of the Buddha's stories as simple fables or parables, without the framework of developed Jātakas are to be found scattered in the various other books of the Pāli canon. For instance, the *Saṁyutta Nikāya* has in it a *sutta* under the title *Sakunagghisutta* or *Sakunovadasutta,* which says that a monk should remain in his own area, i.e. his native beat (in other words, the four *satipaṭṭhāna*s). To express this teaching, a fable of a quail and a falcon is narrated. And it is the same fable that gets developed in proper Jātaka framework in the *Sakunagghi Jātaka* (No. 168) in the *Jātakatthakathā*. Another case in point would be the stories found in another book of the Pāli canon, the *Cariyapiṭaka*. Likewise, there are other fable-narratives scattered in various other books of the canon. They are to be found even in the canonical *Piṭakas*. For example, the *Sukha-vihari Jātaka*, the *Tittira Jātaka*, and the *Khandhvatta Jātaka* are present in the *Cullavagga*.

In each of the narratives, the *bodhisattva* is the central figure. In this sense, the Buddha is both the narrator and an important character of the narratives. Each narrative opens with a preface that explains the narrative context or situation in the life of the Buddha, and then the story narrated takes us back to some particular experience of the *bodhisattva*. The core meaning of his experience is rendered in the form of *gāthā* or verse. In the end, the Buddha identifies the different characters in the narratives in their present birth. The genesis and development of each Jātaka narrative, including the Jātaka fable can be seen in five stages:

(a) The narrative context (*pacchuppanna-vatthu*), which presents the background and the conditions that produce the narrative;

(b) Narrative of the past (*atīta-vatthu*), which delineates a story from a former life of the *bodhisattva;*

(c) Introduction of and perfect placing of the Jātaka verse (*gāthā*), which suggest the practical, religious or moral discourse of the narrative;

(d) Interpretation and explanation of the verse (*veyyākaraṇa*); and

(e) Relation of the characters of the stories of the past with the present characters, including the *bodhisattva.*

These five stages are common to all the fables and also the non-fable narratives found in the Jātakas. In the *Sigāla Jātaka* (No. 148), the narrative context describes the *bodhisattva* faced with the greed and desire of his followers when he lived at Jetavana. He is upset with the lust for gold among his men and states,

> This is like as when thieves break into the city of an emperor; I will unfold the Truth straightway to these Brethren, to the end that, subduing their lusts, I may raise them to *arahatship*.
>
> — *The Jātaka*, 1990: 314

The narrative context makes it very clear why there is this need for the Buddha to narrate a story from his previous birth in which he was a *bodhisattva*. This story would shed light on the present experience of the Buddha with his friends:

> Desire is like poison in food, like the itch in the skin, like a viper, like the thunderbolt of Indra, ever to be shunned, ever to be feared. Whensoever desire arises, forthwith, without finding a moment's harbourage in the heart, it should be expelled by thought and reflection — like as a raindrop rolls at once off the leaf of the lotus. The wise of former times so hated even a slight desire that they crushed it out before it could grow larger. And so saying, he told this story of the past.
>
> — *The Jātaka*, 1990: 314-15

In order to instruct his followers about the inimical consequences of the lust and desire, the Buddha tells them the story of the Jackal (*bodhisattva*), who got entangled in the carcass of an elephant, because of his lustful thought that:

> This carcass is both meat and house to me, and wherefore should I leave it?

The greed of the Jackal (*bodhisattva*) proved costly for him when the summer winds shrank the hide of the elephant and trapped him inside its dark interiors. Later, rains loosened up the hide a bit, and he somehow escaped; though, in the process, he lost all his hair.

Next, the message of the narrative is brought to the listeners by way of a *gāthā* (verse):

> Once bitten, twice shy. Ah, great was my fear!
> Of elephant's inwards henceforth I'll steer clear.

The next stage of development in the fable is where the Buddha explains the implication of the *gāthā* to his followers:

> Brethren, never let desire take root in the heart but pluck them out wheresoever they spring up.

In the last stage of the narrative, the Buddha identifies the character in the story of the past:

> Having preached the Four Truths (at the close whereof those 500 Brethren won *arahatship* and the rest won varying lesser degrees of salvation), the Master identified the Birth as follows: — "I was myself the jackal of those days."
>
> — *The Jātaka*, 1990: 315-16

Through narratives such as these, we come to know about the Buddha's varied experiences before he attained the Enlightenment. They suggest not only an imagined life. In fact, Buddha's historical life as Gautama depends a lot on these narratives. They are composed in Pāli, the sacred language of the Buddhists, though later they were also rendered in Sanskrit.

The 547 Jātakas are compiled in an arrangement of 22 *nipātas* or books. The arrangement of the narratives suggests a great sense of design, which depends upon the number of *gāthās* (verses) a particular story contains:

> The division is roughly founded on the number of verses (*gāthās*) which are quoted in each story, thus the first book contains 150 stories, each of which quotes only one verse, the second 100, each of which quotes two, the third and the fourth 50 each, which respectively quote three and four, and so on to the twenty-first with 10 stories, each of which quotes 80 verses, and the twenty-second with 10 stories, each quoting a still large number. — *The Jātaka*, 1990: xxiii

The Jātakas are remarkable not only for their religious discourse and for reflecting the pre-eminence of the Buddha and explaining the Buddhist doctrines. They are also famous for their relation to the folklore, their expression of the social life and customs of ancient India. Not necessarily all the Jātakas were told by the Buddha or his disciples, nor is it certain that the entire collection of the Jātakas is purely Buddhist. As the Jātakas grew in bulk with their popularity among the people, they assimilated in their content popular tales, ancient mythology and narratives from the older religious traditions. A case in point is the fact that little less than half of the stories in the *Jātakamālā* are not from the Jātakas.

Āryasura compiled a Sanskrit version of the Jātakas, the *Jātakamālā* (*Garland of Birth Stories*). It is an abridged version, and contains only 34 stories. The date of composition is again uncertain and ranges from 200 BCE to fourth century CE. The genre of *campū* (the mixed form of prose and verse) is wonderfully exploited here. The work is the first version of the Jātakas in a non-Pāli language. This version became very popular in the subsequent periods of early Indian history. The Chinese pilgrim I-Tsing mentioned it among the works he found popular in India during his travels at the end of the seventh century CE.

The *Jātakamālā* is not simply an abridgement of the Jātakas. It has an identity of its own very much like the *Hitopadeśa*, which is conspicuous among all the various recensions of the *Pañcatantra* for the new narratives it has added, which were not to be found in the original work. Fourteen of the 34 stories in the *Jātakamālā* are not to be found in the original Jātakas. Āryasura's collection seems to have been guided by the single motif of compassion that the *bodhisattva* shows can be reached through perseverance by refining our passions. For instance, the story No. 15 "Lord of Fishes" delineates the *bodhisattva* born as the chief of the fishes living in a certain lake. The lake is beautiful in which a shoal lives happily. They are gifted with the guardianship of the benevolent *bodhisattva*, who teaches them the secret of happy and compassionate life. Life goes on happily until the drought strikes the place, and the lake faces the threat of complete dryness. The water level goes alarmingly down. The heat is killing and the wind is piercing. Various birds of prey and a pack of crows wait on the bank of the lake expecting the lake to become completely dry so that they feast on the fishes. The *bodhisattva* is moved to utmost compassion at this.

> Grieved by compassion and heaving a long and deep sigh, he looked upwards to the sky and spoke the following words: "As truly as I do not recollect, however pondering, that I ever did harm to any living being, not even in the highest distress, by the power of this truth may the King of the *deva*s fill the water-basins with the water of his rains."
>
> — *The Jātakamālā.* http://www.borobudur.tv/jataka_015.htm (accessed on 15-2-2007)

It is a touching portrayal of the magnificence of compassion. Thus, this Jātaka tale incorporates the religious discourse of Buddhism.

As already mentioned, a number of the Jātaka fables have been represented on the *stūpa*s and other sacred monuments, and the significance of these ancient scriptural monuments in India as illustrating the fables, and determining their historicity, is enormous. Today these representations are of great archaeological value. In fact, it is because of works on these monuments that we can know that the Jātakas not only existed in the third century BCE but enjoyed great popularity among the Indian people. Scenes from the Jātaka fables are found sculptured in the carvings on the railings that surround the relic shrines of Sāñcī and Amarāvatī, and more particularly those of Bharhut. At Bharhut, the titles of several Jātakas are inscribed over some of the carvings.

These reliefs prove that the birth stories were considered a part of the sacred history of the Buddhism. Narratives from the *Jātakamālā* are depicted on the Ajantā frescoes, which date to sixth century CE. The aim of carving the birth stories in verses, then, was to spread the message or doctrine of universal salvation in a form that attracted the common people. Each of the carved narratives presents a necessary perfection that a *bodhisattva* must attain to achieve enlightenment.

The historicity of these representations depends to a great extent on the writings of Fa-hian. After Buddhism reached China in about CE 67, he was the first person to make a pilgrimage to India in CE 399, which lasted for 16 years. When he visited Ceylon (CE 400) he saw at Abhayagiri representations of the 500 bodily forms which the *bodhisattva* assumed during his successive births, and he particularly mentions his birth as Sou-ta-nou, a bright flash of light, the king of elephants, and an antelope. All the *bodhisattva* illustrations that he saw in India and Sri Lanka he has rendered in his work *Foe-Koue-Ki.*

The representations of the *bodhisattva* are not only impressive for the discursive concepts they illustrate but also for their aesthetic value. While the fables represented are clearly discursive, as they depend for their meaning on some idea specific to Buddhism, at the same time they delineate aesthetic beauty. There are various *mudrās* or postures in which the *bodhisattva* is represented.

While the fables in the Jātaka exist within the framework of religious discourse, the *Mahābhārata* fables combine the Vedic mythology and the ancient political systems.

Fables find a place in the *Mahābhārata* in the tradition of the Vedic mythology, but the characters chosen, the situations developed and the discourses put forth in the fables expand the Vedic paradigm to include a political system.

> The device to use fables was somewhat non-Vedic in nature. The works on Vedic rituals ignore the fanciful story of any lucky victim like the goat, etc. But in the *Mahābhārata*, the non-Vedic animal tales and Vedic legends find place side by side. — Kawthekar, 1965: 125

The fable is used in the epic to impart political and worldly wisdom. For instance, Bhīṣma narrates the famous fable of a mouse, who acts cleverly to save itself from the cat, the mongoose, and the owl. The stories, at times, suggest political and war strategy to the characters and hence influence the development of action. The contracted fable that inspires Aśvatthāmā to murder the sleeping children of Draupadī is also very prominent.

Aśvatthāmā is shocked to learn the details of the combat between Bhīma and Duryodhana, which has left the latter mortally injured. This enhances his frustration to answer the deceptive practices of the Pāṇḍavas in the battlefield in the same coin. In particular, he is uncontrollably angry at the way they killed his father, and injured Duryodhana. After the battle, as the sun is setting, Kṛpācārya, Kṛtavarmā, and Aśvatthāmā halt under a huge banyan tree for rest. As they are fatigued the former two fall asleep, but Aśvatthāmā could not sleep for sadness, anguish, and a longing for revenge:

> He was listening to the noises that the nocturnal birds and prowling beasts began to make as the night advanced. He was turning over in his mind how to execute his promise to Duryodhana.
>
> On the branches of the banyan tree, under which the three warriors were resting, hundreds of crows roosted. They were all quiet and asleep until a big owl came and began to attack the birds one after another and kill them. When Aśvatthāmā saw the nocturnal bird of prey tear the helpless crows, he got an idea. The crows that could not see at night flew round

> and round helplessly and fell victims to the owl that attacked them violently.
>
> "These wicked Pāṇḍavas and the Pāñcāla that killed my father and all their supporters can easily be killed by us, if we surprise them when they are sleeping in their tents at night even as this owl is attacking these blind crows. Thus can I avenge the deeds of foul play they have practised on us. I am deeply indebted to this bird of prey from whom I have received the teaching. There is no offence in adopting plans to suit one's altered circumstances. If we can lawfully attack an enemy, when his army is tired or when his forces are scattered, why then should not we, who have lost our armies, attack our enemies when they are asleep? There can be nothing wrong in it. Indeed it is only thus that we can punish and defeat these Pāṇḍavas who have achieved successes through foul play. We have no other course open."

Aśvatthāmā makes up his mind and wakes up Kṛpācārya to inform of his new strategy of attack.

The narrator establishes a perfect analogy between the slaughter in animal world that Aśvatthāmā witnesses on the tree and the slaughter in human world that Aśvatthāmā performs by killing Draupadī's sons:

> After having done this deed, the like of which had never before been considered possible among kṣatriyas, Kṛpācārya, Kṛtavarmā and Aśvatthāmā came out of the tents and set fire to the camp. When the fire spread, the sleeping soldiers were awakened and fled hither and thither in confusion, even like the crows on the banyan tree under which they had rested in the forest, and they were mercilessly slaughtered by Aśvatthāmā.
>
> — *The Mahābhārata* (Section 94) http://home.att.net/~gitaprasad/mahabharata.htm. (accessed on 6-11-2006)

The *Mahābhārata* is a compendium that also includes such fables, and legends, and myths. The significance of the *Mahābhārata* in the fable tradition of India has always been acknowledged. After the Jātakas, it is the *Mahābhārata* which has provided the framework and inspiration for the subsequent development of the fable in India. Holtzmann in his *Das Mahābhārata* claims that in the book 12 of the epic we may actually trace the elements of the precursor of the *Pañcatantra* (in Winternitz, 1977: 335). Maurice Winternitz, on the other hand, argues that the fable verses of the *Tantrākhyāyikā* go back in origin to the *Mahābhārata* (335).

The fables in the *Mahābhārata* are included in the *parva*s like "Ādi," "Vana," "Karṇa," "Śānti," "Anuśāsana," and "Aśvamedhika." As mentioned earlier, the fables are a part of the huge corpus of legends and folk materials that were later included in the epic. For instance, "Śānti-Parva," which is the most significant section in the epic in terms of the fable literature, is actually a huge interpolation.

> The narrative progression is placed on hold almost from the first page. Instead we get a long and winding recapitulation of Brāhmanic lore, including weighty treatises on topics such as kingcraft, metaphysics, cosmology, geography, and mythology. There are discussions of the Sāṁkhya and Yoga philosophical schools, and mentions of Buddhism. It is apparent that the Śānti-Parva was added to the *Mahābhārata* at a later time than the main body of the epic.
>
> — Translator's "Introduction," *The Mahābhārata*, Book XII. http://www.mahabharataonline.com/translation/index.php (accessed on 10-1-2006)

P.N. Kawthekar, in his essay, "Fables in Mahābhārata", discusses two reasons for the inclusion of fables in the epic:

(a) The popular literature was recorded in the great epic under the title of *itihāsa-purāṇa*. Along with the ballads and heroic legends, some popular folk tales were also incorporated in the work. Fables consisting of beliefs, customs, and traditions of common people were made ready for the people; and

(b) Along with the *itihāsa*, full of heroic deeds, the elements of political wisdom were inserted in the *Mahābhārata*; so the fables teach alike the political and worldly wisdom.

While the *Mahābhārata* may have been the precursor of the *Pañcatantra* fable as some critics of the epic claim or it may be one of the most popular carriers of Indian culture, however, as a single work of fable literature the *Pañcatantra* is unrivalled. It has not only remained enormously popular as an entertaining and instructive text for centuries, but has also influenced many other literary works of the world as no other text has ever. The *Pañcatantra* attributed to Viṣṇu Śarmā is one of the most influential texts in world literature, a fact borne by its worldwide translations. It is known as *Kalila wa Damna* or *Anvar-i-Suhayli* or *The Lights of Canopus* in Persian; *Kalilag and Damnag* in Syriac; *Kalila and Dimna*, also *Kalilah and Dimnah*, or *Kalila wa Dimna* in Arabic; and *The Fables of Bidpai/Pilpai* (in various European languages). It was originally a collection of fables written in Sanskrit, in *campū* (mixed prose and verse) form. The original text is long lost. Scholars assume it might have been composed about in between 300 BCE and CE 570. The exact dating of the work is a matter of debate. However, the lower limit (CE 570) is decided by the date of its translation into Pahlavī. The upper limit of its creation is traced back to 300 BCE, because of a reference, in the introductory verse of the text, to Cāṇakya or Kauṭilya, the author of the *Arthaśāstra*, who was feared and admired as the great political strategist and thinker. He was the prime minister under Candragupta Maurya, who ruled between 321-297 BCE.

However, based as the *Pañcatantra* is on older oral traditions, its antecedents probably go back to the origins of Indian language and culture. We have already insinuated its connection with the fables present in the Jātakas and the *Mahābhārata*. In chapter 4, we would explore the intertextual connections of the *Pañcatantra* fables with those in the Jātakas and the *Mahābhārata*. The scholars who have shown interest in the *Pañcatantra* and pursued reasearch on it like Johannes Hertel, Theodor Benfey, Franklin Edgerton, and Ludwik Sternbach, all agree that it was in existence not earlier than the third century BCE, because of its reference to the *Arthaśāstra*; as the age of Cāṇakya is 300 BCE. In the same vein, it cannot be dated later than 500 BCE, because the Persian king Nushirwan ordered its translation whose own period was CE 531-79, and by that time it must have already been a famous work. The fables contained in the work perhaps influenced the Greek collection of the fables, *Aesop's Fables*, and were in turn influenced by it through interchange of stories along trade routes.

The *Pañcatantra*, in one version or the other, has been known throughout the world. King Khosrau Nushirwan of Persia is connected in an important way to the history of the *Pañcatantra* and, to some extent he deserves the credit for the work's worldwide popularity. He was very impressed with Indian stories and had a special fascination for the *Pañcatantra*. The king sent an emissary to India to bring back a version of the *Pañcatantra*. Subsequently, the work was read out and explained to the emissary by his Sanskrit teacher. This is precisely the reason why even the forms of the proper names in the later versions in the Pahlavī sound Sanskritic. In fact, there is a legend about the Persian king and the Pahlavī translation of the Indian book of fables. This legend is narrated by Ibn-ul Muqaffa, who translated the Persian translation of the work into Arabic. Later on this legend was included by the famous Persian poet Firdausi in his *Shāhnāmeh*:

> Anushirwan the Just, Emperor of Persia from CE 531 to 579, was in the habit of consulting sages and physicians. He sent one Barzui [Burzoe], a well-known physician to Hindustan to bring back a wonderful grass which he had read about in an Indian book. The grass, spread upon a dead man, would bring him back to life. The Emperor sent three hundred camel-loads of gifts to the Indian Rājā, through Barzui (Burzoe). The Rājā was very helpful, and Barzui searched in the valleys and the mountains for the grass. Not finding it, he went to an old Sage, who claimed to have made a similar vain search for the grass. The Sage advised that the story should be taken figuratively. The "grass" was Wisdom, which would revive a "dead," that is, an ignorant person. The Wisdom was contained in a Book called Kalila, and that Book was in the Rājā's Treasury. The Sage advised Barzui to get hold of the Book.
>
> On Barzui's request, the Rājā gave him the Book, but would not allow him to copy it out. Barzui took the trouble of learning the Book by heart, chapter by chapter, so that he could later set it down in writing. In this way, he made a complete copy of the Sanskrit text, and took it with him to Persia. There it was translated by one Buzurmihir, and later into Arabic.
>
> — in Balasubrahmanyam, "Introduction," The *Hitopadeśa*, 1989: 17

Therefore, it was under Nushirwan's orders that Burzoe, a learned physician of Persia translated the *Pañcatantra*. Through the medium of various other translations, the most important of which are those in Syriac and Arabic, the work reached different parts of the world. It entered into the literature of West Asia, Africa and Europe. By the sixteenth century, the work was known in Greek, Latin and Hebrew that became the source of its translation into many other European and Slavonic languages. The work came to be known in England under the title *Pilpay's Fables.* In the words of Franklin Edgerton,

> the English version came from an Italian version of a Latin version of a Hebrew version of an Arabic version of a (lost) Pahlavī version of some (lost) Sanskrit version of the original *Pañcatantra.* — Ibid.: 18

The claim of the critics of the work that no other work has travelled worldwide as much as the *Pañcatantra,* except the Bible, is very much true. Apart from the whole work reaching different places, there are also instances of the individual fables travelling to different regions of the world. The fable of the sage and his mouse-daughter found in the *Pañcatantra* III.13, for example, is popular in Burma as *The Bridegroom for Miss Mouse,* and is found in the collection titled *Burmese Folk Tales.* Similarily, in Korea it is known by the title *The Rat's Bridegroom* included in the *Folk Tales from Korea* (Barthakuria, 1992: 17-18). Again, the story of the monkey and crocodile in the fourth book of the *Pañcatantra* has found its way to Central Africa and is included in *Magic Drum,* a collection of Central African folk tales, with an improvisation that the baboon is befooled by a hippo. According to Hertel, the *Pañcatantra* is available in more than 200 versions in over 50 languages, more than 35 of which are non-Indian languages.

A nineteenth-century European folklorist, J. Gorres has beautifully described, by an analogy, the genealogical journey of a particular fable of *Pañcatantra* that travelled around the world through its translation in Arabic, Persian, Hebrew, Greek, Latin, Old French, and eventually in English:

> It sprang originally from the Indian mountains whence from primeval days it took its course as a little rivulet, and flowed in a westerly direction through Asia's wide fields, and,

> while it proceeded for thousands of years through space and time, always spreading more and more in reaching us. Out of it whole generations and many nations have drunk; and having passed to Europe with the great tide of population, it is now also in our day and generation supplied to such a considerable portion of the public, that in regard to its celebrity and the magnitude of its sphere of influence, it reaches the Holy book, and surpasses all classical works. — quoted in Blackburn, 1996: 495

The fable of the Brāhmaṇa and the Mongoose from the *Pañcatantra* is one such tale, which has travelled everywhere as a narrative about the killing of a loyal animal. In the West, this narrative got the acclaim as the story of *Llewellyn and his Dog* (Blackburn, 1996: 494). The story also appears in 18 versions in 10 different languages in modern South Asia. It is also narrated right from Mongolia to Malaysia. It is popular in the form of the Jewish oral narrative tradition in Egypt and Morocco. A Druze version is well known in Israel. It is also found in Russia, in Mexico, and as an anecdote in the United States.

The date of the work goes so far back in time, but it is as modern today. Or else, it would not undergo the never-ending process of cross-border mutation and adaptation by the contemporary adapters and editors who still attempt to fathom, simplify, and represent it. This shows the continuing relevance of the work. Some of the attempts by the modern writers to adapt the *Pañcatantra* and also to translate the adaptations in different languages are to be found in a great number, like the following

(a) *Kalila and Dimna, Selected Fables of Bidpai,* retold by Ramsay Wood (with an Introduction by Doris Lessing), Illustrated by Margaret Kilrenny. New York: Alfred A. Knopf 1980.

(b) *Kalila and Dimna, Tales for Kings and Commoners, Selected Fables of Bidpai,* retold by Ramsay Wood (with an Introduction by Doris Lessing). Vermont, USA: Inner Traditions International, 1986.

(c) *Animal Tales of the Arab World* by Denys Johnson-Davies. Cairo: Hoopoe Books, 1995.

(d) *Kalila und Dimna, oder die Kunst, Freunde zu gewinnen, Fabeln des Bidpai,* erzahlt von Ramsay Wood (Vorwort von Doris Lessing). Freiberg: Herder/Spektrum, 1996.

The *Pañcatantra* was written essentially as a text of political discourse. The fables are in prose, but as in the case of the Jātaka fables, the central message is uttered in the form of verse. It is a comprehensive discussion, through an inter-woven series of fables (and also a few non-fable narratives), of the Indian principles of *rājanīti* (political science), for the use of the princes who are expected to succeed to the throne. The work discusses various political praxis under a well-artciulated design of five sections, which is suggested by the title of the text, *Pañcatantra* (five tenets):

(a) *Mitrabheda* (On Sowing Dissent Between Friends)

(b) *Mitrasamprāpti* (On Gaining Friends)

(c) *Kākolukiyam* (The Crow Empire)

(d) *Labdhapraṇāśam* (On Regaining Losses)

(e) *Aparaikṣṭikarakam* (Inconsiderate Action)

The course of events that lead to the composition of the *Pañcatantra* is also very interesting; the idea behind the composition of the work is itself presented through a small narrative. King Anantaśakti of Mahilaropya has three sons, Bāhuśakti, Ugraśakti and Anantaśakti, who are averse to learning. The king is naturally concerned as a father and as a king about the princes. He summons his ministers for a meeting, and the ministers suggest to him Viṣṇu Śarmā as a *guru*, the one who has mastered all Śāstras. Thus, Viṣṇu Śarmā sets out to compose the *Pañcatantra*, which contains all the knowledge contained in Śāstras, but which is rendered in a fable form for the princes to take interest in learning. The text covers everything conceivable about politics, administration, and ethics. It comes through as a novel educational experiment, and one that worked really well with the three erring princes. It is only because of both the aesthetic and discursive excellence of the work that fables from the text are still taught in schools worldwide.

As we have seen, the *Pañcatantra* has had a long and continuous history, which is unrivalled in world literature. The original *Pañcatantra* was lost and then re-discovered on the basis of its nearest versions that survived. If we have the privilege of reading the *Pañcatantra* today, it is largely due to the efforts of the three major researchers and critics of the Indian literature, who have not only rescued some important versions from obscurity, but also reconstructed the original *Pañcatantra* after reading through the various versions of the work. Theodor Benfey, in a way, pioneered the research on the *Pañcatantra* with his *Pantschatantra, fünf Bücher indischer Fablen* published in 1859; Johannes Hertel followed him with an excellent discovery of the closest recension of the *Pañcatantra*, the *Tantrākhyāyikā,* which helped a great deal in the reconstruction of the original *Pañcatantra*. His book, *Über das Tantrakhyayika, die kasmirische Rezension des Pañcatantra* was published in 1904. Another name very closely associated with the *Pañcatantra* is that of Franklin Edgerton, who came up with the very influential work, *Pañcatantra Reconstructed: Text, Critical Apparatus, Introduction and Translation* published in 1924, after carefully reading through the different extant versions of the work.

Benfey has studied the movement of this work beyond India to the different regions of world literature. In the Introduction to his translation, Benfey claims that *Pañcatantra* has influenced the literature of the world significantly more than any other work from India. Hertel has constructed the history of this work on the basis of the critical editions of the important texts and a huge corpus of scientific research work. He sees a greater relevance of the *Pañcatantra* to the modern folklore studies. In fact, he claims, in the Introduction to his translation, that after working on the work he has established the very foundation of the science of comparative folklore. Equally influential is his argument that the *Tantrākhyāyikā* was a treatise, and it closely adopts the praxis of the Indian *Nītiśāstra*. The composer of the work, he contends, adhered to the subject of *nīti* or policy in it. Again, it is he who claimed that the work was written in Sanskrit in Kashmir.

The textual history of the *Pañcatantra* has been quite an eventful one. That is why Edgerton calls this subject as his "pilgrim's progress of the *Pañcatantra* versions" (Edgerton, 1915: 45). The original text, the "primary work" is of course accepted by the critics and the scholars involved in this field as untraceable. However, whatever knowledge has been gained about the work on the basis of verifiable evidence could help in the reconstruction of that original work composed by Viṣṇu Śarmā. This evidence has been provided by the still existing earliest redactions of the work. Earlier, there existed what is now called *Textus Simplicior* that was considered the primary *Pañcatantra* for a very long time, which was subsequently challenged with the discovery of the *Tantrākhyāyikā*. Likewise, there are many recensions to be found in the different parts of India and the world, and tracing the original *Pañcatantra* is both a taxing and a curious journey. The work has developed over many centuries with many interpolations and subtractions, and has taken different colours from the popular sentiments of the times. Following Franklin Edgerton (*The Hindu Beast Fable in the Light of Recent Studies*) and Maurice Winternitz (*A History of Indian Literature*), we can discuss the genealogical history of the *Pañcatantra* in the following phases.

The Original Pañcatantra, or 'Urpañcatantra

The text is considered lost, and the entire knowledge about it — its form and content — is based on its descendants. It was composed probably in the third century BCE by a Vaiṣṇavite brāhmaṇa, Viṣṇu Śarmā. It consisted of an introduction and five sections, each called *tantra*. There is an interesting reason given by its critics and scholars for the loss of the original text. It was the popularity of the work, they say, which might have been responsible for its loss. The work became enormously popular, and this created the ever-increasing demand for different versions from different parts of India, and its translation into almost every language. In the process, it is believed, the original version of the *Pañcatantra* was lost.

The first scholar and critic to research on the lost *Pañcatantra* was Theodor Benfey. In his two-volume work on the *Pañcatantra* (*Panchtantra: Fünf Bücher indischer Fablen, Märchen und Erzählungen*, Leipzig, Brockhaus, 1859), he (a) gives a history of the *Pañcatantra*, in all its versions and offshoots both in and outside India, and (b) for the first time makes an attempt to trace the history of the individual story and fable motifs found in the various versions of the *Pañcatantra* — one of the earliest examples of comparative folklore studies that is "the comparison of the different versions or outgrowth of the same story themes" (Edgerton, 1915: 44).

But in Benfey's time many of the versions that later became available like the old Syriac version of *Kalila and Dimna*, and the Sanskrit *Tantrākhyāyikā* — two of the oldest and possibly the best representatives of the original *Pañcatantra* — did not exist. Subsequent researches by scholars have thrown new light on the possibility of the reconstruction of the original work.

A new chapter was added to the *Pañcatantra* scholarship with Hertel's *Das Pañcatantra* (Berlin, 1914). It is a meticulous and excellent account of the wandering of the *Pañcatantra* fables. It's "a complete history of the *Pañcatantra* and all its outgrowths" (Edgerton, 1915: 44), which includes a brilliant survey of the versions outside India that descended from the Arabic *Kalila and Dimna*, which is a translation of a Pahlavī translation of a Sanskrit version, both of which are lost, which existed in the sixth century CE.

In the twentieth century, Franklin Edgerton made a valuable contribution in establishing the lost original *Pañcatantra*. Edgerton pursued the most ambitious task of reconstructing the lost original Sanskrit text by an exhaustive comparison of the most important versions. He compared the various versions and analysed the inter-relationships among them, like the *Tantrākhyāyikā*, the *Southern Pañcatantra*, the *Nepalese Pañcatantra*, the *Hitopadeśa*, the poetic versions in the *Kathāsaritsāgara*, and the *Bṛhatkathāmañjarī*, the *Textus Simplicior*, the *Pañcākhyāna* and the important offshoots of the Pahlavī versions. The usual methodology followed by him was that he divided the texts into the smallest possible units, which made possible the comparison of the materials in different versions in terms of their meanings and formal relationships. When Edgerton found "a sentence or verse in identical or practically "identical language, and in the same position, in all the prose Sanskrit recensions, and when its general sense was found in the poetic and translated recensions," he assumed that it was a literal inheritance from the original" (Penzer, 1925: 182-83).

He differs from Hertel in his reconstruction of the genealogy of the *Pañcatantra.* Edgerton believes there are four independent streams of the *Pañcatantra* tradition: the *Tantrākhyāyikā*, the *Southern Pañcatantra*, the *Bṛhatkathā*, and Pahlavī versions, while Hertel, in his *Tantrākhyāyikā* (1909) and *Das Pañcatantra* (1924) argues that there are only two versions, the *Tantrākhyāyikā* and the "k" archetype of all other versions. Hertel further argued that all the existing versions derived from a corrupt archetype "t," whereas Edgerton says both "k" and "t" are as fictitious as Damanaka and Karataka themselves (Penzer, 1925: 183).

There is another point of contention between Edgerton and Hertel. The former confirms that the name of the original work is *Pañcatantra* and that meaning of the work is *Five Tantras*, in which *tantra* means simply a "book" or a division of a literary work. Hertel, on the other hand, argues that *tantra* means "trick" — *klugheitsfall* (Edgerton, 1915: 49).

The Tantrākhyāyikā

It is the recension of the original text recovered from Kashmir, the oldest extant version done in about CE 500. It is not the original *Pañcatantra*, as was believed for some time. Hertel, after a long and arduous research, discovered the text, and edited and translated it in 1910; and all major *Pañcatantra* scholars have depended on the *Tantrākhyāyikā* to get approximate to the original work. Hertel claims the text is "closest to the original of all the Indian versions of the *Pañcatantra* now known to us" (Edgerton, 1915: 53). One proof of this is relative closeness of this text to the Pahlavī translation (which, of course, is lost), on the basis of the latter's descendants. The doubt regarding it being the original *Pañcatantra* is resolved once we come across the numerous interpolations in this text. Therefore, it is more than certain that the original *Pañcatantra* dates earlier than this. Hence, it is true that there existed an original *Pañcatantra* prior to this. However, it is considered the best among all the descendants of the *Pañcatantra* in method and style.

In this earliest version of the *Pañcatantra,* the narratives are placed slightly unevenly among the different sections. The first section has 15 stories, the second section has 10 stories, the third section has only four stories, the last section has just two stories and fourth section has only one story. This apparent imbalance is corrected in the later redactions by adding stories far more inferior to the original *Tantrākhyāyikā* stories. For instance, the frame story of the fourth and the fifth sections has been enlarged, which does not help, in any way, in giving a new shape to the text.

However, it also seems that structurally, the *Tantrākhyāyikā* is the most perfect version of the originally composed work, because it has lesser number of stories, less than 35, and therefore, displays an impeccable form and design, as Hertel opines.

The journey from the *Tantrākhyāyikā* to the present *Pañcatantra* involves some major mutations. There are narratives in the *Tantrākhyāyikā,* which are left out in the modern *Pañcatantra,* like the tale of the onion-thief, who gets triple punishment due to his lack of practical wisdom, found in the fourth section of the text. On the other hand, there are fables from the *Tantrākhyāyikā,* which are retained in the modern-day *Pañcatantra,* but not without some modification, for example, the narrative of the wicked Jackal and the wary Fox in the third section of the *Pañcatantra* (Barthakuria, 1992: 7-8). These are later eliminations and additions. Hertel says,

> Thus, for example, if a story does not occur in all the versions, but only in some of the old versions, it remains doubtful

> whether we can include it in the text of the primary work. Reversely, it is not impossible that an old story may have found place just in one of the latest versions of the *Pañcatantra*. — quoted in Winternitz, 1977: 351

Even more so is the case with the epigrams or the narrative stanzas. It is very difficult to say whether they were a part of the original text or later interpolations. Hertel believes that they have been added later (quoted in Winternitz, 1977: 351).

The Pahlavī Translation and its Descendants

We have already discussed the significance of the Pahlavī version done by Burzoe or Burzoyeh, and the circumstances under which he carried it out. He was an erudite scholar and translator. He had also translated a large number of other narrative works into Persian, but the most important of them was the *Pañcatantra* (which he translated probably in CE 570), that he probably called *Karataka* and *Damanaka*, following the two jackals that play a very important role in the first book of the *Pañcatantra*. Like the original text it is also lost, and again like the original text its form and content are determined on the basis of the later translations from the Pahlavī into Syriac (done by Bud in about CE 570 under the title *Kalilag wa Dimnag*) and into Arabic (done by Abdullah Ibn-ul Muqaffa in about CE 750, under the title *Kalila wa Dimna*), and further the European versions done from the Arabic translation. This text is very valuable for the researchers of the *Pañcatantra*, because it proves that the Indian version used by Burzoe was not at all different from either the original *Pañcatantra* or the *Tantrākhyāyikā*. The connection of his version to the two oldest Indian texts of the *Pañcatantra* is far closer than any other Indian version.

As discussed, Burzoe's version is known only through its descendants, especially the Syriac and Arabic versions, which took the work to medieval Europe. This work survives today in various other versions, the most important of which is the thirteenth century CE Latin translation of John of Capua; this text exercised definite influence on Ibn Zafar's *Consolation Philtres for the Man of Authority*, which is a collection of wisdom lore dramatised by a group of fictitious characters (Winternitz, 1977: 352).

The Bṛhatkathāmañjarī and Kathāsaritsāgara Versions

The *Pañcatantra* can be found next — not the complete work but its extracts — in the Kashmirian *Bṛhatkathā*, made somewhat earlier than the eleventh century CE, which became subsequently lost, and was later found included in the two metrical redactions in Kṣemendra's *Bṛhatkathāmañjarī*, which was a translation into Sanskrit, made in the first half of the eleventh century CE, and Somadeva's *Kathāsaritsāgara*, which was written between CE 1063 and 1081. The original *Bṛhatkathā* (*Great Story*) by Guṇāḍhya was a Prākṛt poem and did not contain any narratives from the *Pañcatantra*. It is on the basis of these two redactions of the Kashmirian *Bṛhatkathā* that critics claim it contained the extracts from the *Pañcatantra*. According to Hertel, after the *Tantrākhyāyikā*, these two redactions, along with the original Kashmirian *Bṛhatkathā*, are characterised as one *Pañcatantra* line, the other being the south Indian and the Nepalese versions, described later.

Scholars, especially Hertel, believe that Kṣemendra handled the original work with greater freedom, often interpolating from the *Tantrākhyāyikā* materials which the original Kashmirian *Bṛhatkathā* did not have. This makes it of lesser value than Somadeva's work. Somadeva's version of the *Pañcatantra* was found in his work, *Kathāsaritsāgara*, the actual name most probably was *Bṛhatkathāsaritsāgara* or *Ocean of the Streams of Bṛhatkathā* (*Great Story*) (Edgerton, 1915: 55).

At the same time, Somadeva's version is distant from the original, as it has passed through two translations. Even the verses, which in all other older versions are preserved well, are affected here. Nevertheless, the form is very ancient and the essence of the stories is well preserved.

Southern Pañcatantra and the Nepalese Pañcatantra

These two versions, along with the *Hitopadeśa*, can be historically traced back to an abstract of the *Pañcatantra* text, which probably existed during the time of Kālidāsa, that is, fifth century CE. Hertel calls the source of these two versions and the *Hitopadeśa* as "n-w"; it contained a quotation from Kālidāsa's *Kumārasambhava*. The southern *Pañcatantra* is a short abridged selection "for instruction of the boys who have learnt little" (Winternitz, 1977: 341). It is an intentional recast like the *Kathāsaritsāgara*. It is an exact imitation of its source text. There are a few new insertions like those in Somadeva's version, the *Kathāsaritsāgara*, but it preserves the verses of the original quite well; the prose text is, however, abbreviated.

It is available in a south Indian manuscript, and hence it is called Southern *Pañcatantra*. Hertel believes that this version originated from a north-western abridgement prepared after the seventh century CE. This text is very crucial to the scholars and editors of the *Pañcatantra*, because it resembles the *Tantrākhyāyikā* very closely, so it could be used for the reconstruction of the original *Pañcatantra* text. Also, this text has issued forth many popular redactions, and has been instrumental in the circulation of the work. Like the south Indian *Pañcatantra*, there are many other extant abridged recensions like the one by M. Haberlandt, and the critically acclaimed *Das Pañcatantra* by Hertel.

The Nepalese *Pañcatantra* and the *Hitopadeśa* together form a development from the same abstract that formed the basis of the Southern *Pañcatantra* (Edgerton, 1915: 58). The Nepalese *Pañcatantra* is preserved today as an ancient manuscript. However, it has only the verses of the original *Pañcatantra*. Its redactor for some reason not known today omitted the prose stories altogether, though it preserves the verses in their original order. Like the Southern *Pañcatantra*, it is also an abridged recension. But it is in metrical form, and is, therefore, unique in itself. This work like the Southern *Pañcatantra* can be traced back to a north-western text. Hertel believes this and the other metrical versions have laid foundations for the new redactions in Sanskrit and the vernaculars. "It is also probable that the stanzas were copied so that they could become aid to memory for the purposes of oral narration" (Winternitz, 1977: 342). Critics opine that this version is closest to the *Hitopadeśa*.

The Textus Simplicior and the Pañcākhyāna

These are evidently the Jain versions of the *Pañcatantra*. Unlike the *Bṛhatkathā* version and the Southern *Pañcatantra*, which contain only abstracts of the *Pañcatantra*, these are the expanded forms of the original work. The title, *Textus Simplicior* sounds uncharacteristic but it was adopted by the critics for want of another name. Edgerton has argued that it was compiled most certainly before CE 1199, because it was used by Pūrṇabhadra for his version, but not before the tenth century CE. Hertel argues that Pūrṇabhadra was a Jain monk, and his version was entitled *Pañcākhyāna*. He wrote his work under the patronage of King Soma. It is considered the most correct, and the most popular *Pañcatantra* text of north-west and central India.

The Hitopadeśa

The *Hitopadeśa*, which can be roughly translated as the *Counsels That are Beneficial*, was composed by Nārāyaṇa as a textbook for teaching the sons of Sudarśana, the king of Pāṭaliputra. Some critics, like Edgerton, believe the work was compiled in Bengal. The title itself indicates the aim of the work. It is meant to impart, through the fables, instructions, ingenuity in speech, and skills in politics. Though the *Pañcatantra* is its primary source, it has autonomy of its own, which is the reason why it is the most popular recension of its source text. In fact, of all the recensions of the *Pañcatantra,* it is most well known as an independent text:

> The *Hitopadeśa* is the first instance we have met — if we except Kṣemendra, which contains a few interpolations apparently from a *Tantrākhyāyikā* text — of a composite version, that is one which is consciously and deliberately undertaken to fuse several texts, or parts of them, into one.
>
> — Edgerton, 1915: 60

Nārāyaṇa has used the same version of the *Pañcatantra* that influenced the Southern *Pañcatantra* and from which the redactor of the Nepalese *Pañcatantra* drew the verse, but he could develop it into a work of its own renown.

The work was composed between ninth and fourteenth century CE (Winternitz, 1977: 359). The author was patronised by one Dhavalacandra. A manuscript of the work found in Nepal is dated 1378, which gives a fair idea that the work must not have been composed after this date. The Nepalese *Pañcatantra,* especially the verses contained in it, draws on it. Not only this, in fact, it is the north-western version of the *Hitopadeśa* that served as a model for the southern *Pañcatantra.* The work soon became accessible in various parts of India. It found its way to Europe in its translated version in English and French. It first appeared in English in the translations of Dr Charles Wilkins and Sir William Jones, which was done very soon after the discovery of Sanskrit literature in the West in the eighteenth century.

The *Pañcatantra* is the source of most of the narratives in the *Hitopadeśa*; Nārāyaṇa has included 56 out of the 71 motives of the *Pañcatantra* tales in the *Hitopadeśa* (Sternbach, 1960). Two hundred forty-one or about one-third of the didactic stanzas in the *Hitopadeśa* can be traced back to the various versions of the *Pañcatantra* (Sternbach, 1956: 119). Hence, the *Pañcatantra* is the greatest single source of the *Hitopadeśa*. However, Nārāyaṇa has not limited himself to the *Pañcatantra*. He is actually a great compiler, who has selected and formatted materials from different sources. In fact, he also mentions that he has also used another work as a primary source. The identity of this other source book is not known. However, as far as the *gāthās* are concerned, the major source other than the *Pañcatantra* is Cāṇakya's compendium or compendia of aphorisms collected and compiled in India and elsewhere under numerous titles. As far as the discursive stanzas of the *Hitopadeśa* are concerned, this one source has been very significant.

> Of the 557 stanzas quoted in all the main editions of the *Hitopadeśa* no fewer than 160 stanzas or part of them, i.e. nearly one-fifth, were borrowed by him from Cāṇakya's compendia. — Sternbach, 1956: 119

The *Hitopadeśa* is, indeed, not a mere imitation of the former. Of the narratives in the text, 10 are not found in the *Pañcatantra*. Not only this, Nārāyaṇa has completely omitted the fourth section, Labdhapranāśam, of the *Pañcatantra*. Again, the verse passages are used more regularly in the *Hitopadeśa* than in the *Pañcatantra*, a good number of which are by Nārāyaṇa himself. There is a major alteration as far as the structure of the entire composition is concerned. Instead of the five books of the *Pañcatantra*, *Hitopadeśa* has four: "Mitralābha" (Acquisition of friends), "Suhṛdbheda" (splitting of friends), "Vigraha" (War), and "Sandhi" (Peace). This work has inverted the order of the first two books of the *Pañcantantra,* made two sections of the third book of the *Pañcatantra,* which is called "War and Peace," and has included the contents of the fifth book of the *Pañcatantra* in these two sections, while excluding its frame story and intercalated narratives. The warring animals are not the Owls and the Crows but the Flamingo and the Peacock with their supporters. The narratives have been altered and the frame-narrative of the fourth book has been created anew. Narratives from different sections of the *Pañcatantra* are given place in the fourth book. At the beginning and the end of each of the books, in this work, there exists a dialogue between the teacher and the princes, whereas in case of the other versions, this interaction occurs only in the *kathāmukha.*

The *Hitopadeśa* very closely follows its source book *Pañcatantra,* in its method and intent. Like the *Pañcatantra,* the work begins with an introduction and invocation to Śiva, and then upholds the power of knowledge and wisdom. Not only this, it sets the main frame story in the similar fashion as its predecessor. Instead of Anantaśakti, we have in *Hitopadeśa* a king named Sudarśana. His sons are equally averse to learning and knowledge, as are the princes in the *Pañcatantra.* There is, however, a difference to be noted in the beginning of the work, which is that this time the king also listens to a poem on knowledge and wisdom, and the speaker, in the course of the poem deliberates on youth, riches, and thoughtlessness as injurious. The king grows pensive reflecting on his stupid sons and calls a meeting of the scholars, and, consequently, Viṣṇu Śarmā takes the responsibility of teaching them polity and practical wisdom. With amazing optimism, he promises to teach the stupid princes within a span of six moons.

The fables in the *Hitopadeśa,* like those in its source book, are composed primarily to suggest a thought or idea. Each fable is meant to illustrate the right way of doing things by example, or the wrong way, by giving warning. For example, the way of making friends and the importance of friendship is demonstrated by the manner in which the Crow, the Tortoise, the Deer, and the Mouse help each other. The Tortoise is saved from destruction by the three others, who live afterwards in peace and happiness. This is the frame-narrative of the first section, and the message in the words of the narrator is that

> Men of friendly disposition, though destitute of means and wealth, speedily bring matters to a successful end like the Crow, the Tortoise, the Deer, and the Mouse.
>
> — *Hitopadeśa*, 1924: 10

Thus, the *Hitopadeśa* uses fables for teaching moral and practical wisdom. There is a great deal of universality about what the fables communicate. The cropping up of differences, disputes and misunderstandings between the Lion and the Bull, who had been friends, suggests how friendship can be broken and turned into enmity by evil, guile, and lies. War is depicted through the battle between the Geese and the Peacocks. In this war, both armies suffer enormous and irretrievable loss, after the great example of valour is shown on both sides. Peace is revealed in the manner in which the damage and destruction caused by the war is repaired by the skilful brilliance of the ministers, who are appointed to look into the differences and the disputes between the warring powers, and work out a solution. Apart from the frame narratives, the intermediary stories too discuss relevant issues of human concern.

All these redactions of the *Pañcatantra* agree remarkably in their form and content. Therefore, they corroborate the fact that there is a single work, the original *Pañcatantra*, from which all of them have descended. Hertel concludes that the *Tantrākhyāyikā*, which is the only complete text, gives the best impression of the original *Pañcatantra.* In fact, so complete is the former, he argues, that is not possible to decide whether the original text be named as *Tantrākhyāyikā* or *Pañcatantra.* There is an ambiguity about whether it is a case of a single text being known by two names, or they were indeed two different works. In the introduction to the *Tantrākhyāyikā*, the author describes his work as *Pañcatantrāṇi*, but the title of the work is distinctly given as *Tantrākhyāyikā* in the colophon (Hertel, *Panchatantra*: Harvard Oriental Series, vol. 14, 1908: 143). But, the work has received its greatest popularity in the world under the name of *Pañcatantra.* Hence, it is appropriate to consider that there was an original *Pañcatantra* text, and the *Tantrākhyāyikā* has been discovered as its oldest version. At the same time, it is also true that generally speaking, what is true about the *Pañcatantra* is also true about the *Tantrākhyāyikā*, and vice versa.

All this debate about the historicity of *Pañcatantra* is not an isolated case in the Indian literary or intellectual tradition. This debate is initiated by the modern scholars of the work. Traditionally speaking, in India the concept of authorship or fixity of textual identity has never been given any importance. A text, though composed by an individual, has always been considered as developing cumulatively with additions and omissions whenever required.

> Literary authorship has always been a matter of small consequence to the Hindus, and plagiarism is a concept which would have no meaning to them. They have always felt as free to deal with the works of others as with their own. Consequently, all versions of the *Pañcatantra* certainly differ from the original in the addition of certain stories, or in the omission of others, or in both respects.
>
> — Edgerton, 1915: 51

Therefore, all the versions are intentionally reconstructed in a significant way. Benfey, who has researched well into this matter, comes with curious observations. He claims that

> the original text rested on a basis of Buddhism, and that in the course of time it underwent a number of important changes . . . in consequence of these changes, a German translation made in the fifteenth century from a Latin rendering which was based upon an earlier Hebrew version represents the original text more nearly than the existing Sanskrit form.
>
> — quoted in Wortham, "Preface," The *Hitopadeśa*, 1924: vii

Though mostly the verses are left unchanged the narratives are almost rewritten. "They tell the same stories but in a wholly different way," says Edgerton. For example, an abstract is made from a story; a story is retold in an "easy-going language, long-winded manner by a later narrator" (Edgerton, 1915: 53). In some cases, even the original prose narrative has been rewritten in a narrative verse.

2

Fable as a Discourse in the Indian Narrative Tradition

> The princes grasp the essences through these five *vidyās* in the stipulated period and become extraordinarily smart in worldly affairs as well as in the basic knowledge needed for running a kingdom's politics. Since then, the *Pañcatantra* has come to be known as the one education medium for those ignorant of deep knowledge contained in Śāstras, Upaniṣads, and Purāṇas. — *The Pañcatantra*, 2006: 14

IN the Indian tradition, a narrative has an epistemological status. A story is committed to a serious social and cultural objective. Beginning with the *Ṛgveda*, a long and ever-evolving narrative tradition has seen the birth and development of numerous genres and modes of story-telling, but the notion that stories are narrated primarily for discursive functions has remained as constant as ever. Any new narrative genre is only recognised as another mode of discourse.

> The Indian tradition has accepted *ākhyāna*, narrative, as a mode of both constituting and transmitting knowledge. . . . Literature for us is not an end in itself. It must serve larger ends. — Kapoor, 2005

The dissemination of the stories was helped by the fact that they were a part of the oral tradition, and hence, the composed narratives either used the elements from the folk tales or became absorbed in the folklore. Almost all the narrative texts include portions from the knowledge-texts such as *Arthaśāstra* or *Nāṭyaśāstra*, which makes it evident that the story was just another method to take the discourse contained in these texts to the people at large. The fables also give the impression of a narrative genre conceived principally for the dissemination of the knowledge of Śāstras:

> The parable, or the fable, which is only the same thing under another name, has always been the favourite Eastern method for conveying instruction . . . story, with an underlying moral, comes natural to the Oriental mind . . . so in a vast and miscellaneous literature, such as the classical literature of India, we should naturally expect to find instruction and wisdom conveyed under this form.
>
> — Wortham, "Preface," The *Hitopadeśa*, 1924: vi-vii

The Upaniṣads, the Brāhmaṇas and the Āraṇyakas, the Purāṇas and the Itihāsas, there is not one narrative composition that does not consciously develop an epistemology. And which is precisely the reason why works like the *Mahābhārata* have been read primarily as knowledge-texts, and are equated with the Vedas.

> The *Mahābhārata* is not only a Veda; it is so important a Veda that to read it is to dispense with the need of reading other Vedas. — Hopkins, 1993: 369

The fables contained in the Jātakas, the *Mahābhārata*, the *Pañcatantra* and its various recensions, apart from being overtly and suggestively mimetic constitute discourses that are political, religious, social, philosophical, cultural, and literary. Even the animal narratives in the *Chāndogya Upaniṣad*, though their form is not as completely developed as the fables in the Jātakas, the *Mahābhārata*, and the *Pañcatantra*, exploit the metaphor of animal lives for the representation of *jñāna* (knowledge). It is very interesting to note that the narrative of Satyakāma uses animals like bull, a flamingo, and a swan for discursive instruction. Such use of animal characters in a composition as old as the Upaniṣads had been greatly responsible in attributing a discursive role to the latter narratives of the Indian tradition.

The *Pañcatantra* alone makes direct references to all the great Indian thinkers of various fields like Pāṇini, Jaimini, Kauṭilya (Cāṇakya), Kāmandaka, Bharata Muni, and Vātsyāyana. There are also many references to the *Nītiśataka* of Bhartṛhari. Many of the aphoristic utterances in the *Pañcatantra* are attributed either to Cāṇakya or Bhartṛhari. The author first pays his respect and indebtedness to Vācaspati, Śukra, Parāśara, Vyāsa and Cāṇakya, and then he says that Viṣṇu Śarmā, after he has gone through the essence of the *Arthaśāstra* and other Śāstras, the Upaniṣads and the Purāṇas existing in the world, has written, in the five books of the *Pañcatantra*, a thoroughly delighting lesson. Indeed, describing the *Pañcatantra* as a fabular version of the various Śāstras would not be an overstatement.

The fables in the *Pañcatantra* produce small sections from the various philosophical, political, and literary texts. These discursive sections are judiciously placed within the narrative framework of a fable. To begin with the literary discourse, the *Pañcatantra* makes it evident that the *Nāṭyaśāstra* is truly the fifth Veda, a Veda that mediates between the philosophy and the folk. This goes on to show that Bharata's discourse on dramaturgy had become very popular about the time Viṣṇu Śarmā composed his work. Listening to the serious discourse of music, including the accurate descriptions of *rasa* and *bhāva*, from the mouth of the foolish Donkey is amusing, but there is point behind this that the reader should not miss.

It is in the fifth book of the *Pañcatantra* that a fable features the Jackal and the Donkey, who clandestinely enter a garden to eat the sweet cucumbers. It is a beautiful full moon night, and, inspired by the romantic ambience, the Donkey wants to sing. The Jackal tries to stop the Donkey, and rightly so, because the Donkey could only bray, which would wake up the watchman. Seeing the Donkey adamant to sing, and failing to reason with him, the Jackal crosses over to the other side of the fence, in order to save himself from the guard. The Donkey brays and awakes the watchman, who beats him roughly. Therefore, it is a bit incongruous that the Donkey Uddhata should talk about the *Nāṭyaśāstra* and the Indian music.

Nevertheless, it is this incongruity that makes the use of a detailed description of melody and music prominent. As is the wont with the *Pañcatantra*, the description from the *Nāṭyaśāstra* is presented as a serious discourse, and is not confused with the foolishness of the Donkey. The Donkey lectures about the seven notes of music, the 49 *gama*s, 21 *mūrcchana*s, 49 quavers, three *mātrā*s, and three *tāla*s. He goes on to discuss *yati*, *āsya*s, *rasa*, and *bhāva*. Then, he makes a direct reference to Bharata Muni and the 185 divisions of music that he enumerated. Like a serious critic of music and literature, the Donkey Uddhata rates the *Nāṭyaśāstra* as the fifth Veda.

If we accept that the *Pañcatantra* was a popular text, as the critics of the work have suggested with examples, then the numerous references to philosophers and intellectuals from the Indian tradition makes a curious case of what is considered today intertextuality. The texture of the fables in the *Pañcatantra* is replete with quotations and references from numerous thinkers and their texts. This only goes to show that as a part of the oral tradition these texts were in constant circulation in the social sphere. Even a discipline as intellectual and abstract as philosophy is talked about in the *Pañcatantra*. In the second book of the *Pañcatantra*, the mouse Hiraṇyaka lectures about the Indian Grammarian Pāṇini, and

Jaimini, the sage who composed the Indian philosophical system, the *Mīmāṁsāsūtras*.

One reason why we find discussions about the Indian knowledge systems in the fables of the *Pañcatantra* is that the text had to teach the various disciplines through these limited number of fables. Hence, the author-narrator thought it essential to intersperse portions from the various knowledge-texts, which he illustrated through the fables. For example, the author-narrator has put the entire gist of an important Buddhist concept in the mouth of the cunning Cat in the third book of the *Pañcatantra*:

> Oh! This world is inessential; life is ephemeral, the pleasure of the company of relatives and near and dear ones is like a dream; the upkeep of family is part of a grand magic show. Therefore, there is nothing real apart from *dharma*.
>
> The body is mortal, wealth will not stay forever; one moves around with death surrounding him, therefore one must enrich himself with *dharma*. — *The Pañcatantra*, 2006: 219

What the cunning Cat says, especially in the first paragraph, is an important tenet of the Buddhist philosophy

> according to which the world is without any substance like a dream or a magic world or a mirage. The Buddhists also proclaim the dictum that all in the universe is *kṣaṇika* or momentary in character. — Barthakuria, 1992: 134

Though the fable may have animals as speaking and acting, the form is held on the serious message that takes it forward. The form of the fable does not shadow the message; rather it intensifies the discursive content expressed by the narrator and the author. The *Pañcatantra*, for instance, is obviously a guide to success in politics. The first book shows how a king might lose his best and trusted friend, ally, and counsellor if he is not careful about the treacherous wiles of a courtier; the second book shows how the unity of wise and prudent friends can save them from a powerful enemy; the third book reveals how a political trick can make a plan against an enemy, superior in material strength, successful; the fourth book shows how a person, in a hopeless situation, can escape an almost certain death through an impudent deception; and the fifth book delineates the mischief produced by careless and hasty action.

It is very apparent to the reader as to what has been intended for him/her, for instance, in the story of the Crocodile and the Monkey or the Donkey in the Lion's skin. In fact, the element of discourse is more pronounced in the fables than in other narratives, so there is no difficulty in placing the Indian fables within the knowledge-defined narrative tradition of India. On the other hand, it is extremely easy to talk about the fables contained in the Jātakas, the *Mahābhārata,* the *Pañcatantra* or the *Hitopadeśa* as subjects of knowledge, because their narrative contexts, the conditions of their narration, also suggest religious, political, or social discourses.

The first three books of the *Pañcatantra,* with some exception, foreground political discourse, especially their frame-narratives, whereas, the fourth and the fifth books proclaim worldly wisdom. However, critics believe the two kinds of discourses are interrelated and complement each other. Hence, they cannot be put in different categories; it is because, worldly wisdom is as important as the knowledge of the politics to attain power and success. That is the reason why in the *gāthās* (stanzas) and the epigrams we find political ideology and worldly wisdom alike. As far as the number of aphoristic statements is concerned, the work weighs heavily in favour of the political discourse. Out of the 451 sayings of the *Tantrākhyāyikā,* 205 are about politics, 138 deal with general thoughts of worldly wisdom, and 108 are about moral, philosophical, and religious discourse (Winternitz, 1997: 347).

The Buddha was determined to take the teachings and messages of *dhamma* to the common humanity of the Indian society. So, he made use of story-telling to achieve his purpose. He recognised the faculties and abilities of the folk. Bharata composed the *Nāṭyaśāstra* as the fifth Veda, because the common humanity could not grasp the Śāstras. In the same vein, the Buddha understood that narratives, including fables, would be the best method to disseminate the Buddhist doctrines. This methodology of the Buddha was naturally understood by folk, his disciples, and the future leaders of the *Saṁgha*. As the Jātakas existed in the oral tradition, they assimilated in themselves popular tales, ancient mythology, stories from the older religious traditions, etc. In brief, the Jātakas imbibed the common heritage of the Indian masses. Though the narratives are primarily Buddhist, they do deal with life outside the religious influence. The eighth-century Chinese pilgrim I-Tsing felt

> the object of composing the Birth Stories is to teach the doctrine of universal salvation in a beautiful style, agreeable to the popular mind and attractive to readers.
>
> — Bhattacharya, *Jātakamālā*,
> www.boloji.com. accessed on 6-8-2006

The Jātakas were compiled primarily so that the Buddha's teachings could be preserved for posterity, as they were originally intended. They had become so popular and circulated so much in the society that the monks feared the narratives could be manipulated and a lot of corruption would enter into them. This goes on to show how as a discourse the Jātakas were considered of serious consequence, that their misreading or misinterpretation would do gross injustice to the purpose for which the Buddha first narrated them. The stories delineate the religious discourse of the formative years of Buddhism, but they also shed light on the social, political, and religious life of the people of ancient India.

The primary concern of the fables in the Jātakas, therefore, is to validate the Buddhist discourses. In each fable, the Buddha foregrounds one aspect of the requisite perfections (*pāramitās*) that a *bodhisattva* must master on his or her way to achieving enlightenment. It is generally believed by the Buddhist scholars that in each of the narrative the remaining nine virtues are also embodied, because they inevitably must play their respective supporting parts whenever the *bodhisattva* implements a task of perfection. The *gāthās* in the fables are specifically used to convey that doctrine alone. For instance, in the *Munika-Jātaka* (No. 30), the *bodhisattva* is born as an Ox, Big Red. He and his brother, Little Red, are employed at a squire's estate. His brother complains:

> All the loads that have to be drawn for this household are drawn by you and me, my brother; but all they give us for our pains is sorry grass and straw to eat. Yet here is the pig being fed on rice! What can be the reason why he should be treated to such fare?

> The elder brother, the *bodhisattva*, tells him that the pig is being fattened for slaughter, and, therefore, he gets better things to eat. He goes on to give a discourse on the virtues of contentment, which is an important Buddhist doctrine. Now, if the Buddha had taught the doctrine simply, it would not have made as much effect on the masses as he got by creating a fable around this discourse. The fable ends with the central thought contained in the *gāthā* (verse), which is how each and every fable provides the religious teaching:

> Then envy not poor Munika; it's death
> He eats. Contented munch your frugal chaff
> The pledge and guarantee of length of days.
>
> — *The Jātaka*, 1990: 75-76

Inherently, the fable is used by the *bodhisattva* for didactic purposes. The narrative is focused on resolving a situation or problem caused by the development of conflicting interests. It is the development of tension which holds the narrative together and contributes to the dynamics of the story, and also keeps the listeners of the narrative involved. A successful narrative strategy used by the *bodhisattva* depends on identifying and offering ways out of problems and conflicts that are confronted or pre-empted.

The fable as a discourse in the Indian tradition can be discussed in terms of its historicity, its connections with the folklore, and its use of the contemporary systems of social and political thought. The discursive value of the fables has been quite pervasive throughout. In fact, on second reading, the fables seem so discursive in intent that though they are still pleasant to read, they are more inclined to a pattern of thought they seek to promote. They are primarily meant to enhance a particular aspect of knowledge.

The narrative texts like the *Mahābhārata* and the *Pañcatantra* are firmly placed in the beginning itself in discursive terms. The *Mahābhārata* is spoken by Vyāsa as containing all the knowledge of the Vedas to the extent that what is found in the *Mahābhārata* would be found in all other knowledge texts of the Indian tradition, but what is not found in the epic would not be got anywhere. The centrality of knowledge is stressed in the central framework of *Pañcatantra*. In the introduction to the work (*kathāmukha*) the king Anantaśakti of Mahilaropya asks his ministers the ways to make his sons wise and knowledgeable. The ministers say,

> O king! It takes twelve years to master Grammar. Thereafter Manu's and other Dharmaśāstras, polity by Cāṇakya and others, *Kāmaśāstra* and other scriptures on lovemaking by

> Vātsyāyana and others are taught. Only after mastery in these, one is considered educated.
>
> — *The Pañcatantra*, 2006: 13

It is obvious that any pedagogical text chosen for the princes would constitute all the knowledge texts. And indeed it is so, because the *guru* chosen for the education of the princes is Viṣṇu Śarmā, an old man of 80 years, who has mastered the *Nītiśāstra*, and all other fields of knowledge. He declares the king may exile him, if, in six months, he could not make his sons expert in *Nītiśāstra*. Benfey has argued that the author Viṣṇu Śarmā is no other than Viṣṇugupta, another name of the great Indian political philosopher and thinker Cāṇakya. The text composed by him for the education of the princes, the *Pañcatantra*, contains all the knowledge required. In its most popular recension, the *Hitopadeśa*, there is no ambiguity about the discourses that Viṣṇu Śarmā would teach to the erring princes. The king tells the *guru*:

> Even an insect, if it be on flower, may ascend the head of the great; a stone if consecrated by a man of mighty power becomes divine. . . . Therefore you shall be the instructor of my sons in Political and Social Science.
>
> — *The Hitopadeśa*, 1924: 9

It is mentioned that the king is himself a scholar of *Arthaśāstra.*

Thus, the work was originally meant to train the princes. But gradually it acquired fame as a manual for the training of the youth in general, not merely the royal princes. Hertel calls the various versions of the *Pañcatantra* as "school books." This is proved by the inclusion of the stories from the *Pañcatantra* and the *Hitopadeśa* in the school textbooks in different Indian languages.

The *Pañcatantra* very frequently refers to long political or ethical treatise culled from the various discursive texts. In fact, the work starts with the merchant Vardhamāna giving a long discourse on the merits of enhancing one's wealth. If this seems an example of an exceedingly mundane discourse, then there are many discourses on ethics spread throughout the other fable-compositions. In the frame-narrative of the first book, we get a comprehensive political discourse between two fox-brothers that consists of the citations from the authoritative texts on politics, and the fables that they narrate delineate the political maxims. One of the foxes, Damanaka is worried about the well-being of the Lion king, Piṅgalaka, as the latter has been behaving unusually as a feeble animal, uncharacteristic of a lion, full of fear and discomfort. Whereas, Karataka, his brother, advises him not to meddle in the affairs of the king, and that he should mind his own business:

> Karataka replied, "Brother why should we bother? What is the use of our thinking on this subject?"
>
> A person engaging in futile tasks not of concern gets destroyed the same way as this monkey died a painful death upon drawing out a nail from wood.
>
> — *The Pañcatantra*, 2006: 31-32

In order to counter his brother's philosophy of keeping to one's own matters, Damanaka brings forth a detailed discourse from Śāstras:

> Only they deserve to live whose life is inspiration and means of survival for several others. Otherwise, even birds get enough to eat and fill their belly by mere use of beak.
>
> Among the humans those who have mastered the sciences, have acquired virtues of bravery and earned wealth and have won honours, if for a moment, are considered by the wise as having really lived. Otherwise, even the crow lives a long life and consumes sacrificial meat.

> He who shows no mercy to relatives, to the mute and weak creatures or even to other humans, hardly serves any purpose in life. . . .
>
> What is the good of a man taking birth and snatching the youth of his own mother to grow up to be of no use to anyone nor to bring glory to his family or uphold the flag of his own clan. . . .
>
> Even the blade of grass growing on a river bank is more useful if it serves to save a drowning soul and rescue him from his last minute misery.
>
> Those moving in all circles of people and serving to reduce their misery, like clouds bringing relief from hot Sun, are few in number. . . .
>
> More one should speak where it benefits someone so that its results are seen just as red colour that fixes better on clean white cloth. — *The Pañcatantra*, 2006: 32-34

This discursive harangue goes on and on unabated for a few more pages. It becomes very obvious here that this ethical discourse is addressed, more than Karataka, to the readers beyond the immediate framework of the narrative.

Apparently, the discursive quality of the *Pañcatantra* is very strong and intense. Evidently, the work has gone through as many as 25 versions, and, yet every time it has been read and interpreted through the prism of political thought.

> While the older versions are associated with Cāṇakya or with the Kauṭilya *Arthaśāstra*, attributed to him, in the later recensions Kāmandaka's *Nītisāra* is mentioned and cited as the main authority. — Winternitz, 1977: 354

Though we are dealing with the fable world which is ostensibly fictitious, yet the political life comes across in convincing terms through the narratives. The political system and the power-structures as well as the court life of the times find a perfect reflection in the fables. As far as the *Pañcatantra* is concerned, India was then ruled by monarchs like Nanda that the author mentions. There is also a reference to kingdoms like Gurjaradeśa and Avantī. However, more important for us is the use of contemporary political discourses in the fables, which comes from the *Arthaśāstra*. In terms of the power-structures in a predominantly monarchical system of ancient India, the king's ministers assumed a very crucial role. They played a very important role in decision-making. It is true that monarchy was not democratic and it rested on the absolute powers of the king, yet on important political matters he did wish for a consensus involving the opinions of his ministers and advisers.

The king consulted not one but as many ministers as he could on important policy matters. This is evident from the frame-narrative of the third book, the story of Meghavarṇa and the owl-king in "Kākolukiyam." The very fact that Yudhiṣṭhira, the future king of Hastināpur, is asked in the *Mahābhārata* to receive discourses on polity from Bhīṣma, who lay on the death-bed, goes on to show that it was the duty of the king to keep himself update on political knowledge. In most cases, it was the minister that the king looked up to for keeping himself abreast of the political and ethical principles. For instance, Dhr̥tarāṣṭra depends a lot on the wisdom of Vidura for his political decisions, and his kingdom is eventually destroyed, because he did not heed to the advice given to him by his minister. In the first book, "Mitrabheda," of the *Pañcatantra*, for instance, the system that binds the king with his subordinates is expressed perfectly by Damanaka:

> Without attendants, the king gets no glory and is just like the life-giving Sun which is hidden in clouds.

> Just as the centre of the wheel is connected to the rim with spokes, the same way the king and attendants complete the circle and the business rolls on. — *The Pañcatantra*, 2006: 42

When the lion king Piṅgalaka is scared to death hearing the mysteriously dangerous roar of the bull Sañjīvaka, it is his attendant Damanaka who comes to his rescue. The king is extremely distressed, and is contemplating to forsake his kingdom, and escape to some other forest:

> "Dear Damanaka, I have a heart to leave these woods for it appears an upheaval is in the offing . . . because it appears from now on there is entry of a strange beast in the jungle and one can listen to its loud roar. Probably he is also powerful."

> Damanaka acts here as an able counsellor that any king would be proud to have with him. He is not only gifted with a great foresight and knowledge of the political affairs, but also an insight into human nature:

> Just as bridges are pulled apart due to the velocity of the overflowing rivers, the same way a precious thing is lost to the enemy who is gainer merely because he frightens by noise. Complainants often manage to harm themselves by talking ill of another.

> Damanaka eventually proves to be a great inspirer. The wisdom of the king's counsellor and his ability to inspire the king to perform glorious deeds is well acknowledged in the Indian political discourse. Accordingly, Damanaka encourages his king to face the situation with courage and strength:

> The king who retains his courage and confidence even before a powerful enemy is never defeated. The patient man should not lose courage even before an adverse fate because the sea only swells up with scorching heat which would dry up lesser lakes and rivers.

> Moreover, one who does not waver before adversity or get excited with wealth or frightened by war is a rare child of a fortunate mother in all the three *lokas*.
>
> And yet, "becoming modest after loss of power, being taciturn after losing one's essential character and losing one's self-respect place the person in the category of grass eater without strength, shine or core of life."
>
> And then, "Getting support from others, if one is still unable to firm up, what is the use of the person who is now like a mere body, ornament made of iron only?"
>
> — *The Pañcatantra*, 2006: 42-45

This long conversation between Damanaka and Piṅgalaka unravels the responsibilities of the ministers in dispensing their duties to the king and the state, as enshrined in the authoritative text of politics like the *Arthaśāstra*. It also presents a mirror to the way the king and his ministry functioned in a close relationship in a crunch situation in ancient India. This conversation between the two suggests that the foremost duty of the minister was to advise the king and bring him to the right path when he deviated. This principle is derived from Cāṇakya. It is also said that when the king moves away from the right path, the ministers are to be blamed for not correcting him, and this is exactly what Damanaka wants Karataka to understand. The ministers had to give their important advice, which at times was different from what the king thought. It was important, nevertheless, for the king to take their word.

> Thus, the duties and responsibilities of the ministers in the age of the *Pañcatantra* as in modern times were very great. The success of the king in internal administration and against external enemies greatly depended on the fidelity and the responsibility borne by his ministers.
>
> — Barthakuria, 1992: 59

The third book of the *Pañcatantra* is even more expressive about the critical responsibility of the ministers to the state, especially in the time of emergency. What the text says could be verily accepted as norms that governed the profile of a minister's position *vis-à-vis* the king and state in ancient India:

> As it is understood, at such times the ministers should always come ahead to give advice even when not asked and work out a strategy. At such times of exigency if a minister decided to keep silent he should be considered an enemy who speaks sweetly but hides malice in heart. — *The Pañcatantra*, 2006: 204

The *Pañcatantra* recognises the ability of the ministers in tackling political issues and affairs, and while doing so makes a direct reference to a passage from Kauṭilya's *Arthaśāstra* that lists the five *mantras* of diplomacy:

> (i) The remedies to be adopted at the beginning of an undertaking,
>
> (ii) Having at the command sufficient supply of men and methods,
>
> (iii) Proper division of time and space,
>
> (iv) The remedy against dangers or difficulties, and
>
> (v) The success in the mission.
>
> — Barthakuria, 1992: 59

The third book of the *Pañcatantra*, "Kākolukiyam," is throughout a discourse on the state, its policy, and its machinery in the times of war. As the book begins, the narrator hints at a right kind of policy that state should adopt in the event of external aggression, through the analogy of a person, which is relevant even today:

> The person who out of sloth ignores the enemy moving ahead with abandon, or a disease either, and does not try to

> stall them, he gradually gets killed by that very enemy or disease. He is killed even though strong.
>
> — *The Pañcatantra*, 2006: 203-04

In the second book, "Mitrasamprāpti," the mouse, Hiraṇyaka, expresses the kind of ideology that an individual or a state should adopt while dealing with other individuals or states. The essence of polity, according to him, is to remember the antecedents of the other person or the state before trusting as a friend:

> If one has harmed someone once and tries to become friends again he should be avoided, otherwise the person courts his own death. — The *Pañcatantra*, 2006: 157

In order to give credence to his thoughts, Hiraṇyaka refers to some major thinkers from the Indian tradition. And indeed the reference to the concepts promulgated by these thinkers makes the discursive features of the *Pañcatantra* very strong. To establish his views about the three wings of polity, he takes recourse to the thinkers:

> Cāṇakya opined we must do good deeds; Śaṅkarācārya said one must seek more and more friends, and Bṛhaspati taught the policy of not trusting another.
>
> — *The Pañcatantra*, 2006: 159

Laghupatanaka, the crow, seeks friendship with Hiraṇyaka, because of his vast knowledge, which again validates the importance attached to knowledge in these fables.

Beyond the immediate interest generated by the war between the owls and the crows, the frame-narrative creates a conceptual structure, wherein sections from various authoritative texts are freely quoted. The immediate situation is that the Crow king Meghavarṇa is extremely concerned about the safety of his subjects, as the owls led by their king Arimardan continue to pursue aggression, and every night quite a few of his subjects are killed by the enemy. It is difficult to defend his subjects, because they live on a tree, which is not fortified, and, to aggravate the situation, they cannot see in darkness. He summons his senior ministers, and in the top-level meeting we get a glimpse of the various ways to deal with enemy during war, as enumerated by the Indian political thinkers.

The first minister suggests restraint and buying peace for the moment, and then attacking the enemy once it is made weak by employing different policies. To support his claim, he refers to a tried and tested method employed in the traditional Indian politics:

> In this world the outcome of a war is always uncertain. Hence, one should go to war only when all the three forms of truce *sāma, dāma, bheda* have failed . . . and if these fail, then consider open war. — *The Pañcatantra*, 2006: 205

The means of fighting the enemy which are advocated by Kauṭilya in the *Arthaśāstra*: *sandhi* (peace), *vigraha* (war), *saṁśraya* (seeking help), *āsana* (stay put inside a *durga* or fort), and *dvaidhibhāva* (duplicity or double dealing), find reference in more than a few places in the *Pañcatantra*. For instance, the seniormost minister Sthirajīvin prevails upon his king to adhere to *dvaidhibhāva* in order to destroy the enemy, and the king by placing his trust in the policy of this minister eventually tastes victory over the stronger army of the owls. Again, in the midst of the debate between Damanaka and Karataka, on whether or not to ask the lion king, Piṅgalaka, the reason of his trouble, and offer him assistance, we find a reference to this same principle enumerated in Kauṭilya's political theory as mentioned by the minister in the third book, "Sthirajīvin":

> Damanaka says, "today the king sits with his family scared. Therefore, we must approach him, enquire into the reason

> of his worry and advise him pact (*sandhi*) or war (*vigraha*), with the enemy. If not these, I would advise him to stay put and wait and then join the more powerful of his two enemies (*saṁśraya*) and if both of his enemies are equally powerful to live in equanimity with both (*dvaidhibhāva*). I shall suggest to him anyone of these proposals after knowing the exact cause of his worry. — *The Pañcatantra*, 2006: 35

Sthirajīvin, the minister of the Crow-king Meghavarṇa, draws an elaborate analogy between his experiences inside the enemy territory with the various adverse experiences the Pāṇḍavas faced in the *Mahābhārata*. He argues that in the days of adversity, the superior human being would deal with the hardships with fortitude, not getting perplexed by the atrocious present but rather living the hard times with grit and determination. Such a person has the ability to foresee that the difficult present would lead to a pleasant future. Arjuna had to live the life of an effeminate dancer and decorate his hands with jewellery, the same hands that carried the strong bow, *Gāṇḍīva*. Bhīma had to work in the kitchen. Nakula and Sahdeva had to look after the cows and guard the house of Virāṭa. Even Draupadī had to suffer mortification. But all of them persevered well. He draws this analogy as a response to the assumption of his king that he must have suffered a lot in the enemy territory. The king confesses that he and the other ministers had really been worried and anxious about his well-being. This is what the aged minister says after completing this analogy with the Pāṇḍavas:

> It is a sign of mature politics that great men even obtaining to severe difficulties never leave a task in the middle.
>
> Lowly persons of base personality never begin a task; those of medium character leave it midway when adversities strike. It is only the best among them who finish a task begun.
>
> — *The Pañcatantra*, 2006: 256

There is also another analogy with the *Mahābhārata* present in this book of the *Pañcatantra*, which appears before the war between the crows and the owls. The Crow-king and his ministers are drawing out strategies that they would like to adopt for the war. There is a direct analogy between the discourse given by Nārada Muni to Yudhiṣṭhira and the words spoken by Sthirajīvin to Meghavarṇa. The Crow minister does acknowledge the source of his discourse to Nārada Muni. It is about the king being aware of his chief points of weaknesses, which his enemy might exploit to defeat him:

> There are 18 prime weak targets the enemy can impinge upon to control the king, and these should be guarded, and there are 15 that are weak points of personal nature. One who keeps a watch over these is able to prevent calamities.
> — *The Pañcatantra*, 2006: 212

Some of the weak target points enumerated by Nārada Muni and re-told by Sthirajīvin to the Crow-king are: the minister, the priest, the army commander, the prince, the gatekeeper, the chief of the army staff, the chief of the elephant department, treasury, border security, and so on and so forth. Some of the weak target points related to the personal life of the king are the chief queen, the queen mother, the chief of spies, the *guru*, the bodyguard, the courtesan, etc.

For knowledge on the war and the methods employed as means of combat during the war, the fables in the *Pañcatantra* freely draw from the *Arthaśāstra*, especially Cāṇakya's strong recommendation of a strong fortress. There are many examples in the Indian history how the fortress as a defence was actually adopted by numerous kings:

> In ancient India, fortresses played a very important part in defence. A king could easily resist his enemies by taking shelter in a fortress. We learn from the history of Alaudin Khalji that the Hindu king Hammīradeva effectively resisted

> his mighty enemy Sultan Alauddin for a long period by adopting this strategy. But when there was a great scarcity of food inside the fort, he came out and fought valiantly with the enemy and died. — Barthakuria: 1992: 68

There is an exact analogy to this in the third book of the *Pañcatantra.* One of the reasons why the Owl-king is more powerful is that he and his subjects live inside the invincible fort of a mountain cave. Though the Crow-king himself has the luxury of a fort-like construction in the depth of the foliage of a tree, most of his subjects live on the foliage or around it, and perish to the attack of the owls at night. Therefore, Prajīvin, one of his wise ministers rightly suggests *āsana* (living in wait inside a strong fort, and wait for the right moment to attack) as a strategy to deal with the stronger enemy. Using an appropriate analogy he says that a jackal staying at an appropriate spot can even defeat an elephant, but his moving away from its favourable place might even make a dog stronger than it. He sums up this very important concept developed by Cāṇakya in the following words:

> Hence let us strengthen our fort, recruit more soldiers and mass foods and weapons and work on ditches, etc. to be ever prepared for war. If victory comes after such a fight it is glory and kingdom. And even otherwise we attain to heaven being true to political morality. Moreover, it will become difficult to owls to meet us when we are externally well defended even if weak positioned compared to them. The wind cannot uproot creepers anyhow. — *The Pañcatantra*, 2006: 209

In the second book, the Mouse-king Hiraṇyaka dwells in an underground fortress having many tunnels and winding escape routes that provided security to him all the times, in the event of any exigency. Here, the narrator gives a very poignant discourse on the utility of the forts for a king and his subjects:

> A king without a fort is easily controlled just as the toothless snake or a sober elephant. A single soldier can fight hundreds from inside a castle. — *The Pañcatantra*, 2006: 153

In the first book of the *Pañcatantra,* the popular narrative of the clever Hare and the foolish Lion, Bhasuraka establishes a historical perspective to the construction of the forts. This fable narrates the very popular tale of the Lion king Bhasuraka who ruled over a jungle. So that the king does not kill his subjects in the jungle indiscriminately for food, it is decided that the subjects would offer an animal each day to save this widespread killing. One day it is the turn of the witty Hare, and he traps the Lion Bhasuraka through a false account of another lion who claimed to be the real king. As the Hare prepares to tempt Bhasuraka to a well in whose reflection he would show Bhasuraka the other lion, and provoke him to jump on the supposedly other lion in the well, he tells the following discourse on fort. His description establishes the mythological history of the concept:

> What is not achieved by a number of horses and elephants is possible once one is inside the fort. One archer from inside the castle can target hundreds. That is why politicians always prefer a fort.
>
> In ancient times on Bṛhaspati's instructions Heraṇyakaśipu built a fort with the help of Viśvakarmā. Viśvakarmā even blessed him with success. Since then a number of forts were built by kings on earth. — *The Pañcatantra*, 2006: 86

Apart from erecting fortresses, the *Pañcatantra* draws on implementing other efficient systems of defence enumerated in the ancient Indian political thought, like a well-organised army consisting of cavalry and infantry. There is also an elaborate discussion about espionage in the ancient Indian political thought, which finds a depiction in the *Pañcatantra,* especially in the third book. Kauṭilya says, in the *Arthaśāstra,* that the king should have a well-worked-out espionage system for the defence of his country against the internal and external enemies. He describes, for example, the different types of spies like *tikṣana rasada, śatrin, udāśita,* and *kapaṭika.*

Sthirajīvin, the wise minister of Meghavarṇa, speaks about the crucial part played by the spies in political matters. He informs his king that it is the duty of the spy to mislead some important officers, especially those closely associated with the enemy king to act in a manner that would bring their downfall. Thereafter, gaining a nod from his king, he prepares to get into the enemy territory of the owls as a spy. The Crow-minister poses himself as the great friend of the Owl-king, and after winning the confidence of the Owl-king, he destroys the owls in the most unprecedented manner with the help of other crows. They completely burn down the cave-dwelling of the owls.

The immediate utility of the discourse on war for the listeners of these fables, the princes, and probably the general people of that time, figures in the *Hitopadeśa.* Unlike their source book, the narratives told by Nārāyaṇa involve the princes' participation in the section on war. They take active interest in discourse brought to them in the form of these narratives. They are interested in the discourses on war, because, as they say, the teachings are relevant to their lives as princes. The fact that, at the end of the book, the princes, who have been so averse to learning, could utter a maxim on the war shows the pedagogical effectiveness of the narrative in putting across a serious subject in an interesting manner. At the end, the royal students confirm, by demonstration, that they have perfectly understood the important things to know about the warfare, and thank their *guru.*

Even apart from the war, other political discussions in the *Hitopadeśa* are more distinct than in any other versions of the *Pañcatantra*. The discursive sayings from the Nītiśāstras are disseminated more through the *Hitopadeśa* than any other book of fables in India. The verse quotations are taken from Kāmandaka's *Nītisāra*. The *Hitopadeśa* is indeed a brilliant selection of narratives built around the epigrams that carry forward the political weight of the narratives. "Of the 600 sayings . . . 273 relate to king's politics, 222 to common worldly wisdom, and only 105 have a moral or religious theme" (Winternitz, 1977: 360). For instance, in order to bolster the courage of his brother, Damanaka makes an aphoristic statement, which he quotes directly from the Nītiśāstras:

> It is the mark of a weak man to do nothing for the fear of making mistakes. People do not abstain from eating for the fear of indigestion. — *Hitopadeśa*, 1924: 77

Through the fables in the *Pañcatantra*, we get a glimpse into the court life of the ancient India. The systems governing the life of the kings at the courts are comprehensively depicted in the fables. For instance, the security arrangements of the king in the ancient India are discussed in the frame story of the first book. The Lion king Piṅgalaka, for instance, moved in a quadruple ring (*caturmaṇḍala*). The king had this ring around him all the time when he was on the move. The king was in the centre of the quadruple ring, which was surrounded by his closest and trusted associates, the second circle. The third ring comprised of the servants called *kākaravas* (the word *kākarava* means those people who can immediately give the hint of danger to the king). The security guards or officers known as *kimvṛttas* formed the fourth ring. In the third section of the *Pañcatantra*, there are references to *aṅgarakṣaka* and *sayyāpālaka*.

The work contain more references to the hierarchy at work in the royal courts in ancient India. In the frame-story of the first book, again, a gatekeeper regulates the entrance of visitors to the royal court with the cane that he holds in his hands. Damanaka, the Fox, wanted to enter the court in order to meet the king. The King Piṅgalaka ordered the gatekeeper to remove the cane and let him enter. Damanaka bowed to the king, and sat on the seat that was meant for him.

In the frame-story of the third book, the Crow-king Meghavarṇa bows with respect to the old and wise minister Sthirajīvin. Now, it was a protocol observed then, and it had also been a traditional practice for the king to bow down to a veteran minister. Sthirajīvin had been a minister since his father's time, and hence he followed the tradition by showing respect to him.

This does not mean that the fables in the *Pañcatantra* are only concerned about the royal life. They adequately delineate the legal and civic discourse that concerned the common populace of India, which are relevant even today. In the fables, we find the critical discussion of the laws governing landed property, tanks, wells, trees and temples, and the like. The *Pañcatantra* points to the fact that there existed well-defined laws in ancient India. The narrative of the Hare, the Sparrow and the Cat, in the third book of the *Pañcatantra* discusses some of the property laws operative in ancient India.

In the hollow of a certain tree, the Sparrow Kapiñjala lived with his friend the Crow. They were highly intellectual and often talked about gods, sages, kings, *maharṣis* and the scriptures. Once, Kapiñjala went out, as usual, with other birds for food but did not return for very long. His neighbours and friends grew very worried; they gradually accepted, with a sad heart, that he had probably been captured by some hunter. After some time the Rabbit came to the tree and made the hollow his home. One day Kapiñjala arrived from nowhere, and was extremely upset when he saw his house being occupied by a stranger. A dispute arose between the two, and Śuśa, the Rabbit, protested when asked by Kapiñjala to vacate his abode. He made his arguments sound very legal: "This house is not yours but mine only. Then why do you speak in hard tones? It has been said:

> After establishing, the pond, the well, the temple, and the tree do not belong to any one individual . . . it is the norm that the person living at a place for 10 years becomes its owner without the need of any proof or evidence. Such continued use itself is the proof of ownership."
>
> — *The Pañcatantra*, 2006: 218-19

The logic put forth by the Rabbit sounds quite modern. The laws that the Rabbit quotes have been picked up directly from the Smṛtis. The Smṛti text says that ownership is lost forever if the owner donates an asset as public property.

The fable delineates the settlement of this dispute, as practised in the ancient India, in detail. Both the Hare and the Sparrow decide to approach a legal expert, one who could correctly interpret the Smṛti rule. Thus, the fact that both the parties show respect to the laws enshrined in the law books reveal that the legal aspect is seriously pursued in the story. The legal expert they contact has mastered the Dharmaśāstras, and can judiciously give the verdict in terms of the scriptures.

Though the immediate interest of the fable is sustained by how the Cat, a reputed lawyer, dupes both of them and devours their flesh, it scores some important points about the legal discourses in the ancient India, and the respect people had for law. The Rabbit and the Sparrow know that the Cat is their natural enemy, but they do not avoid going to her, as her knowledge of the law is widely acclaimed. The Cat ends up being cunning and motivated by self-interest, which is nothing surprising about the *Pañcatantra* animals. At the same time, the narrative is more interested in drawing out the legal knowledge from her. She says,

> The man who judges merely to retain his honour among men or does so motivated by greed or fear only chooses the path of hell. The judge telling a lie for the sake of gaining animals incurs the sin of killing five people; those giving wrong judgements to get a cow incur sin of killing ten people; for a girl the killing of hundred people; and for another person of one thousand people.
>
> A person sitting in a court of law not speaking the truth, that is, not taking a clear stand should be removed from the court because truthfulness itself is justice. It is the duty of the king to verify the truth of an event.
>
> — *The Pañcatantra*, 2006: 221

As in other cases, a mere substitution of the king with the modern state would make the modernity of the fable quite apparent. The fable points to some specific laws in the discourses of eminent lawgivers of ancient India like Yājñavalkya, Nārada, and Kātyāyana. In ancient India, these thinkers framed certain important laws about the right of possession over a plot of land, or wealth. Yājñavalkya says that when a person does not resist an encroacher for 20 years from enjoying his land, the encroacher becomes the virtual master. Nārada contends that the right by occupation is the strongest point in deciding the ownership over a plot of land, and any document in the support of the previous owner is useless. Kātyāyana, on the other hand, says that the person, who currently enjoys them, is the actual owner (Barthakuria, 1991: 81-82).

Kauṭilya's connection with the discourse that the *Pañcatantra* foregrounds has been researched extensively by critics like Ludwik Sternbach and Franklin Edgerton. It is essentially focused on discussing the work as approximate to *Nītiśāstra*. The fables convey a need to discuss the *nīti* discourse in its historicity:

> . . . The Indian Fables have got close relation on the origin and development of the Indian Nītiśāstras. In certain occasions fable stories have been composed in order to illustrate compressed pithy sayings of a *nīti* verse, and, sometimes the fables have given occasion for the new composition of the *nīti* verse. — Pathak, 1974: 19

According to Sternbach, *nīti* is "the age-old art of getting along in the world" (quoted in Ingall, 1966: 2), and this is primarily the subject that Viṣṇu Śarmā wants to impart to the erring princes. The avowed objective of the *Pañcatantra* is to teach the "*Nītiśāstra* ("Science of Conduct" i.e. the Art of Administration, Politics), in other words *Arthaśāstra* "the Science of Worldly Advantage" (Winternitz, 1977). The connection of the work with the *nīti* discourse makes it primarily a knowledge-text. Now the scholars are divided about the origin of the *Nītiśāstra* as a discipline. In the beginning, the Nītiśāstras or Nīti kāvyas did not have an identity as a separate genre. The Nīti kāvyas have their source in fact in the entire expanse of Indian literature. It is generally believed that well before Kāmandaka's *Nītisāra* and other texts of *nīti* literature, the discourse was spread over the different texts of early India, in the form of sayings. These were the gnomic and didactic stanzas on polity and on ethics, and practical wisdom expressed, as discursive statements, at different places in the various texts. Subsequently, they developed as a selection from the different compositions of

Indian literature, and then also got absorbed in the folk as popular proverbs:

> Wherever we go through ancient Indian texts we often come across moral precepts or ethical instructions (*nīti* and *upadeśa*), together with guidance on polity (*rāja-dharma*), which may be described as early specimens of *Nītiśāstra* or *Nīti Kāvya* as some orientalists put it. — Pathak, 1974: 16

The Vedas and the other Smṛti and Śruti texts of the Indian intellectual tradition are the ultimate sources of the practical knowledge on the administrative policy, especially the statecraft, found in the *Pañcatantra* fables and those in the *Mahābhārata*.

> In search of the origins of the Indian Nītiśāstras, it is observed that the main object of the *nīti* sayings is to instruct the fundamentals of social (in other words, moral) and of political life which are found explicit in so many verses and passages of the Vedic Saṁhitās, and later on in the Brāhmaṇas. — Pathak, 1974: 18

In the long oral traditions of India, Vedic seers, Buddhist monks, Jain *śrāvaka*s, and thinkers of many other religious orders uttered their discourses on polity and administration in verses on different occasions. Later, the discourses given by the ancient Indian thinkers of Smṛti, Arthaśāstras, and Dharmaśāstras were compiled and collected and quoted in different Nītiśāstras as counsel books on polity, ethics, and administration. The elocutions in the Vedas, especially *Ṛgveda*, on general ethics and the human beliefs of Vedic India, moral stanzas in *Aitareya Brāhmaṇa* and the Upaniṣads, the ethical and political concepts uttered by sages or learned characters in the *Mahābhārata* and the Purāṇas, and the *Dhammapada* of the Pāli canon, can truly be held as the sources of the *Nītiśāstra*. There is also a corollary concept of *nīti-dharma*, instructions on polity and statecraft that are given on different occasions in the *Rāmāyaṇa* and the *Mahābhārata* as *rāja-dharma*. In fact, in the two epics ethical virtues and polity are considered as integral to *dharma* (Pathak, 1974: 18).

In the same way, there were various attempts made by the Jaina teachers to collect and compose a large number of scattered ethical texts to impart teaching to the masses, but it can be seen that a lot of sayings in those Jaina Nīti Kāvyas are related not only to Jainism, in the same way as the *gāthās* of the Jātakas and of the *Dhammapada*, though traditionally believed to be the utterances, of the Buddha, do not always seem Buddhistic. So, the Indian *nīti* discourse that has a major presence in the fables of the *Pañcatantra* and those in the *Mahābhārata* has emanated from quite a wide field of early Indian literature. Suniti Kumar Pathak, in the book *The Indian Nītiśāstra in Tibet*, cites Monier-Williams following assessment of how the *nīti* discourse developed over time in India:

> Numbers of wise sayings have, from time immemorial, been constantly quoted in conversation. Many thus orally current were of such antiquity that to settle their authorship was impossible. But occasional attempts were made to give permanence to the floating wisdom of the day, by stringing together in stanzas the most celebrated maxims and sayings like beads on a necklace; each necklace representing a separate topic and authorship of a series being naturally ascribed to men of known wisdom, like Bhartṛhari, Cāṇakya, much in the same way as the authorship of the Purāṇas and the *Mahābhārata* were referred to the sage Vyāsa.
>
> — Pathak, 1974: 20

The knowledge contained in the *Nītiśāstra*, however, is not limited to the abstract theoretical formulations. In the narrative form, they delineate an attitude to individual and social life. The aim of human life as understood in India is attainment of *puruṣārtha* — the fourfold ways of life, which covers life in all its aspects, *dharma, artha, kāma,* and *mokṣa.* Nītiśāstras cover all four aspects of life so that the ethical virtues, like regard for all beings, hospitality to fellow beings, etc. as practised by the *bodhisattva* are *dharma* for a social life; the ethical merits like truthfulness, tolerance, are *dharma* for an individual being, as adequately reflected in the Jātaka fables. While *dharma, artha,* and *mokṣa* are predominant in the Jātaka fables, the fables in the *Mahābhārata* delineate *dharma* and *ārtha.*

In the *Jātakamālā,* righteousness as enshrined in the concept of *dharma* is established by fables like "The Hare":

> The practice of charity according to their power by the Great-minded, even when in the state of beasts, is a demonstrated fact; who then, being a man, should not be charitable?
>
> — The *Jātakamālā*: 6. http://www.borobudur.tv/jataka_030.htm. accessed on 4-1-2004

The *bodhisattva* preaches compassion for fellow beings in the "Lord of Fishes," by his act of empathy for the other fishes in the drying lake. Truthfulness is emphasised, for instance, in the fable of the Donkey in the Lion's skin in *Siṁhacamma Jātaka.* The *gāthā* makes it very apparent that falsehood will lead to trouble:

> The donkey, if he had been wise,
> Might long the green barley have eaten;
> A lion skin was his disguise:
> But he gave a hee-haw, and got beaten.
>
> — *The Jātaka,* Book II, 1990: 76

The Jātakas primarily present ethical and religious discourse, but it is not distant from what we understand as *artha.* Not only are there fables like the one about the Crocodile and the Monkey (*Suṁsumāra Jātaka*) which recommend a lie to save one's life, but also in some cases a fable presents *dharma* and *artha*, as communicated by the *gāthā* from *Siṁhacamma Jātaka* quoted above. Though it is preached that the Donkey should not have adopted falsehood, it is also suggested that it could well have enjoyed the barley had it been successful in hiding its true identity. Thus the Jātaka fables promote both *dharma* and *artha* alike.

On the other hand, though the *Pañcatantra* fables primarily express policies that propagate worldly benefits for a person or a community, which falls within the purview of *artha;* they do foreground *dharma,* though only in some of the fables. In the frame-narrative of the first book, Damanaka tries very hard to make his brother Karataka understand their *dharma*/duty with respect to the Lion king Piṅgalaka. It is their *dharma,* he argues, to show the king the right path at the difficult hour, when he is losing hold over the situation. Likewise, the second fable about the birds in "Kākolukiyam," foregrounds the *dharma* of a king. The birds are extremely unhappy that the king is not following his *dharma*: "our king is a devotee of Nārāyaṇa and takes no notice of us. What is his use when hunters catch us daily, and there is no protection?" (*The Pañcatantra,* 2006: 213). The fable is quite contemporary. We only have to put the modern state in place of the king. The birds further say that the *guru* who does not study the scriptures, and the king who does not protect his subject are violators of the *dharma*.

The *dharma* of the king as delineated in the *Pañcatantra* fables is interestingly quite at one with what the *bodhisattva* puts forth in the *Jātakamālā*. The narrator makes an analogy between the leader of the fishes in the lake, who is *bodhisattva* himself, to such a king who follows his *dharma* of protecting his people in the event of any trouble:

> Owing to these efforts, as well as his knowledge of every expedient, the *bodhisattva* made them forget their habit of

> feeding in the cruel manner of fishes. Duly protected by him, that shoal of fishes came to great prosperity just as a town, when ruled by a king that acts in the proper manner, enjoys freedom from every kind of mishap.
>
> — The *Jātakamālā*: 15. http://www.borobudur.tv jataka_030.htm. accessed on 4-1-2004

Both the Jātakas and the *Pañcatantra* say that the *dharma* of the king is to protect the people. Therefore, the notion of the king concerned about the welfare of his people is centralised. In Jātaka No. 240, *Mahāpiṅgala Jātaka*, the *bodhisattva* dismisses the king who was "like a speck of dust that falls in the eye, like gravel in the broth, like a thorn sticking in the heel" (*The Jātaka*, 1990: 166). In a way, this narrative is very modern. There is a free expression of resistance against the king and a celebration at his death:

> Thousands of loads of wood have burnt him quite,
> Thousands of pitchers quenched what still did burn;
> The earth is dug about to left and right —
> Fear not — the king will nevermore return.
>
> — *The Jātaka*, 1990: 167

Kauṭilya in the *Arthaśāstra* (III) considers the *rājā* as the *dharmapravartaka*, which means the initiator of the *dharma*.

> In the Jātakas, the concept of justice is interwoven with that of the *pañcaśīla*, the five virtues, adherence to which was expected from the king, the common men and women, the Buddhist monks, and the nuns alike. These included abstinence from taking that which is not given, from misconduct stemming from desire (*kāma*), from telling lies, and from consuming intoxicants. — Roy, 1996: 28

The notion of the just and the unjust king in terms of law and justice is equally stressed in the *Mahābhārata*. In the "Śānti-Parva," Bhīṣma puts his views on the political morality of a king through a fable. He gives a discourse on *rāja-dharma* to

Yudhiṣṭhira, Vidura, and Dhṛtarāṣṭra. He narrates the fable of the mouse to delineate the king who acts to save his kingdom from the enemies that surround it.

> Political thought was interspersed with the fables in the *Mahābhārata,* because the subject matter of the Jaya Bhārata was war, and hence the *ekāyana* or *rājanīti* or *yuddhaśāstra* was the essential element of the subject matter in the great epic. The stand of the victorious Pāṇḍavas was to be justified on basis of the tradition. — Kawthekar, 1965: 126

However, generally, for the text as a whole, the *Pañcatantra* fables have their distinct philosophy, which does not go along with the general discourse of the Jātakas. According to Johannes Hertel the term *tantra* in the title of the *Pañcatantra* means "good sense." He coins the German word *klugheitsfall* for *tantra. Klugheitsfall* means "case of good sense" when translated into English. He likewise says, *Tantrākhyāyikā* means in German "Ans Erzählungen von Kiugheitsfallen bestehendes," which when translated into English means "manual consisting of tales of cases of good sense" (Hertel, "Preface", *The Pañcatantra: A Collection of Ancient Hindu Tales in Recension, Called Panchakhyanaka,* 1908). Accordingly, the *Pañcatantra* would mean five cases of good sense. The work employs fables to impart the knowledge of good sense in politics. Hertel considers the work a manual of statecraft in the same vein as the Machiavellian literature. He further explains the work as propagating "artifice" or "case of political prudence." He is so radical in his assertion that he argues that all those stories that do not conform to the superiority of cunningness to stupidity should be marked as interpolations (in Tawney, *Folklore,* vol. 20, no. 4, 30 December 1909: 509).

The concept of *nīti* belongs to a discourse which is diametrically opposed to any convention which regards the practice of virtue rewarded and vice punished as valid. Hence, *nīti* is squarely antithetical to moral discourse as we find reflected in the Jātaka fable. In the Jātakas what is good is governed by the Buddhist principles of right conduct, whereas in the *Pañcatantra* fables whatever is useful in material terms is good. This opposition exists notwithstanding the fact that a few fables in the *Pañcatantra* were adapted from the Jātakas. In the *Kapota Jātaka*, for instance, righteousness of conduct and abstinence from greed is emphasised. The cunning Crow is lured by the smell of food in the kitchen where the Pigeon (*bodhisattva*) has built his nest. It is in the house of the Lord Treasurer. The cook of the house is fond of the Pigeon and offers him the straw basket. In order to gain access to the kitchen the Crow befriends the Pigeon. It is welcomed by the cook who hangs another basket of straw for the Crow. But the Crow has other intentions. He has taken shelter inside the kitchen to devour the meat and fish that very often was cooked there. So, one day he makes an attempt to eat the fish. But, in the process of stealing, he is caught and punished.

In the *Pañcatantra* fables cunningness and deception seldom fail. They are recommended as methods of success. The narrative of the Snake, Mandaviṣa, told in the third book exemplifies this. The Snake wants easy food and in order to catch the frogs living in a pond he entraps one of them by narrating a false story:

> The Snake said, "Brother, how can I now desire food? Because only last night I saw a frog and wanted to catch it for food. Seeing me he was scared and ran to hide among brāhmaṇas reciting Veda-*mantras*. I could not see him and mistaking the foot's toe for the frog, I bit a brāhmaṇa's son, and he died." Then his father cursed me in sorrow: "You scoundrel, you have killed my innocent son. So now for this crime you shall act as a vehicle for the frogs and that will be your only source of livelihood."
>
> — *The Pañcatantra*, 2006: 254

All the frogs, including their king, make a rush for the joyride provided by the Snake. The next day the Snake is able to convince the king to allow him to devour some small frogs as he is tired, and cannot give him a joyride. Gradually he eats up all the frogs. Hence, Edgerton rightly comments that "at any rate, the main purpose of the book was to teach worldly wisdom — especially political wisdom, of a highly unmoral and Machiavellian variety." Hertel believes the general tone of the fables in the *Pañcatantra* is tricky and unmoral, "if not positively unmoral."

Therefore, there is a world of difference between what the fables in the Jātakas and the *Pañcatantra* communicate. The *Pañcatantra* fables belong to a different world view. "None of the stories of the original reveal such marked religious purposes as appear in many Buddhistic and Jainistic stories" (Edgerton, 1915: 50). While compassion is preached by the *bodhisattva* (for example, in "Lord of the Fishes") as a virtue to be attained, it becomes a grave mistake in the *Pañcatantra*. Compassion and mercy that go against self-interest in fact invite condemnation in the *Pañcatantra*. In the third book, the king of owls, who spares the suppliant Crow Cirajīvin, is ruined consequently. If he had followed the advice of his intelligent and sensible minister, Raktākṣa, who suggested that the Crow should be immediately put to death, he would certainly have saved himself and his kingdom. In fact, the Crow Cirajīvin regards Raktākṣa with respect and not the king who had spared his life. After his victory and complete decimation of the owl-empire, he tells the Crow-king:

> Dev, I have not seen anywhere more foolish a crowd than the owls and none more intelligent and knower of Śāstras than Raktākṣa who understood my hidden thoughts and motives well by the simple premise that enemy's servants

> can never do good. The other ministers were simply there for namesake. They had no efficiency.
>
> — *The Pañcatantra*, 2006: 252-53

In this context, Benfey's contention that the fables in the *Pañcatantra* are derived from the Buddhist Jātakas becomes little difficult to accept, unless the stories have been manipulated to serve the respective discourses. As we can see, the fables in the *Pañcatantra* are meant as a manual of politics, and, therefore, they will appear highly incongruous in a Buddhist work, since Buddhist Jātakas, and Buddhism in general, do not attach any meaning to the righteousness of effort for gaining earthly things and earthly power as promoted by the *Nītiśāstra*. In the words of Winternitz,

> Benfey had arrived at his conclusion with regard to the Buddhist origin of the *Pañcatantra*, because he knew only a single text, of one Jaina version, and, on the other hand, because he was able to locate many of the stories in the Buddhistical narrative works, the antiquity of which he has exaggerated. In fact we come across many of the *Pañcatantra* stories in the Jātaka book, and we can hardly say with considerable certainty today that in such cases the Jātaka book has got the stories from an earlier version of the *Pañcatantra*. Thus, for example the Jātakas Nos. 349 and 361 have been taken from the frame-story of the *Pañcatantra*.
>
> — Winternitz, 1977: 350

It is possible that fables in both compositions have adapted the narratives from each other and transformed them in terms of the specific discourses that each promotes. For instance, in the Buddhist version, some *nīti* stories have been transformed into *dhamma* stories and vice versa. Or, in some other cases, the narratives in the *Pañcatantra* that conform to the dominant discourse of the Jātakas appear as exceptions, as for example those narratives promoting *dharma*.

We cannot say with certainty as to which composition has been influenced by the other. What we can say with certainty is that the ethical philosophy of the two is so widely different for them to be so related, without the necessary changes in the discursive statements that the author-narrators put in the mouth of the characters. At the obvious level, meanings expressed by the political characters in the *Pañcatantra* sound like the ethical utterances one would find in the Jātaka fables. But on critical examination, the reader would find that there is a major difference in the world views. In the frame-story of the second book, the kindness towards other beings shown by Pigeon-king Citragrīva, in his self-negating address to the Mouse-king Hiraṇyaka, cannot be the same as the ascetic-moral discourse in the Buddhist texts. Citragrīva seeks not to protect all (animals), which is *ahiṁsā,* but to protect and defend those who have given themselves to his care.

In the same section, Manthraka gives the following advice to Hiraṇyaka:

> Pacified sages advised quietening of desires as the source of personal peace; just as fire does not quench thirst, wealth does not bring the peace of mind.
>
> . . . In this world giving alms is the biggest treasure, no greater enemy than greed, no other jewel than good behaviour and no bigger wealth than contentment.
>
> — *The Pañcatantra,* 2006: 185

No doubt this sounds like a prominent discourse we generally associate with the fables from the Jātakas, but once the reader is aware of the narrative context of the utterance, it becomes clear that rather than being a proclamation of a universal truth, it is influenced by the need to provide a temporary relief to a friend. This passage can be put along the pious utterances by the cunning Cat in the third section, who quotes from the

Dharmaśāstras in order to pretend to her prey that she would not harm them; but eventually she devours both of them.

All the ethical utterances in the third book serve the theme of friendship. The benefit of friendship for evading dangers and achieving political success is emphasised. For example, the Pigeon-king Citragrīva and his people escape the hunter's net because of their unity. It is because of their unity and the friendship of the Mouse-king Hiraṇyaka that they survive. Now, the Crow Laghupatanaka (Light-winged), who has seen their great friendship, asks them to accept him as their friend, and then they add two more friends to their group, the Tortoise Mantharak (Slow) and the Deer Chitrāṅga (Coloured-Body). In one instance, which delineates the utility of friendship, the Deer is caught in the net of a hunter, and the other friends rescue him. Hence, whatever discursive content we have in this section, no matter how ethical it seems, is oriented towards the worldly advantages of friendship.

The fable about the quails in the Jātakas promotes the same motive of unity among kinsmen. It is Jātaka No. 33, the *Sammodamana Jātaka*. In this fable, the *bodhisattva* is born as the leader of the quails. There is a fowler who has created havoc in the community of the quails by catching them in his nets every now and then. The *bodhisattva* suggests to them the way out of this crisis:

> This fowler is making havoc among our kinsfolk. I have a device whereby he will be unable to catch us. Henceforth, the very moment he throws the net over you, let each one put his head through a mesh and then all of you together must fly away with the net to such place as you please, and there let it down on a thorn-brake; this done, we will all escape from several meshes. — *The Jātaka*, 1990: 85

Now, this advice of the *bodhisattva* to his folk is not different from what the Pigeon-king Citragrīva tells his subjects by way of an analogy:

> If the particles of a substance are minute and numerous and of long strands they are able to absorb many shocks if they stick together. Hence one must stay in a group, when weak, in order to meet the exigencies and turn out successful.
>
> — *The Pañcatantra*, 2006: 152

In both the fables, the birds are able to rescue themselves heeding to the advice given by their respective masters. The idea contained in the two fables is the same and so is the narrative detail, but the discursive intent of the two is class apart. In the above statement, the Pigeon-king says unity is important when a group is weaker than its enemy. What is meant is that the fable in the *Pañcatantra* advocates unity for an immediate gain. Though the fable in the Jātaka delineates the immediate benefit to the quails, what it actually promotes is that people should generally not fight among themselves, which is a universal message. It promotes the message of love and compassion among kinsmen and women.

Now, though in their discursive intent the *Mahābhārata* fables complement those in the *Pañcatantra*, especially the fables that are employed in political discourse, there lies a difference. Like the fable about the Pigeon-king that also appears in the Jātakas, the entire frame-narrative of the third section of the *Pañcatantra* comes from the *Mahābhārata* (Parvan X). The attack on the Crow-king, Meghavarṇa, and his subjects by the Owl-king, Arindham, and his army, and the massacre that follows sets the frame-narrative rolling. The same incident sets Aśvatthāmā thinking in the *Mahābhārata*, and he decides to go for a nocturnal attack on the Pāṇḍava camp when Draupadī's sons are sleeping in their tents. What is important to note is that in the *Pañcatantra*, the sole concern is self-protection and victory over the enemy. The ethicality of the means adopted is immaterial so long as earthly success is achieved, which is the innate understanding exuded by all the characters of the fables in the *Pañcatantra*. Even, the Crow-king and his army wreak revenge and destroy the owl empire by using the way of deception.

Quite different is the case in the *Mahābhārata*, where the ethical imperative is adequately discussed before the attack. What the owls did to the night-blinded crows in the darkness is against the *dharma*. Kṛpācārya loses no time to argue with Aśvatthāmā:

> It is wholly wrong. To attack men, who have retired to sleep, has never been done before. It would be an unprecedented crime against the laws of kṣatriya conduct, Aśvatthāmā, for which we are fighting.

Because of Aśvatthāmā's justification of this plan, it appears the world view of the fable comes closer to what the reader sees in the *Pañcatantra*. But it is only momentary. Aśvatthāmā argues:

> These Pāṇḍavas have been guilty of the foulest conduct. They killed my noble and trustful father through a lie. They have killed Duryodhana against the laws of chivalry. I have no doubt in my mind that what I propose to do is quite proper vengeance for all these foul deeds. It is only if I carry out this plan that I can possibly repay my debt to my king and to my father.
>
> — *The Mahābhārata*, Section 94, retold by C. Rajagopalachari. http://home.att.net/~gitaprasad/mahabharata.htm. (accessed on 6-11-2006)

The same argument can be used by Meghavarṇa's ministers for the fraud they would play in order to take revenge on the owls. However, such a need does not arise in the *Pañcatantra*, because, as discussed, there is no questioning of the ethical dimensions of the means. In the *Mahābhārata*, however, the *dharma* is the touchstone. The means adopted by the Pāṇḍavas are justified because they are on the side of the *dharma* in the great war, whereas what Aśvatthāmā does, as what the owls do, stands reprimanded in the epic.

The overall impression that the *Pañcatantra* fables create is definitely that intelligent conduct for self-benefit even at the cost of morality is justified. But having said that it should be noted that there are some fables in the work that do not go along the general discourse in the work. We have already discussed the concept of *dharma* as enumerated by Damanaka. In the second book, "Mitrasamprāpti," Laghupatanaka, the wise crow performs his *dharma* by saving the other birds from the hunter's net. His action represents love and concern for others in the society:

> O birds, this wicked hunter is carrying net and rice grain with him. Do not trust him at all. Consider the rice as worst poison. — *The Pañcatantra*, 2006: 151

Therefore, the fables of the Jātakas and the *Pañcatantra* belong to two different knowledge systems; while the former is a religious and ethical discourse, the latter a *nīti* discourse, that prefers self-benefit over ethics, but there are a few stories that do not conform to these categories, and overlap. Arthur Berriedale Keith says in his *History of Sanskrit Literature*,

> The fable, indeed, is essentially connected with the two branches of science known by the Indians as the *Nītiśāstra* and the *Arthaśāstra*, which have this in common as opposed to the Dharmaśāstra that they are not codes of morals, but deal with man's action in practical politics and conduct of ordinary affairs of everyday life and intercourse. We must not, however, exaggerate this contrast between these Śāstras for in the *Arthaśāstra* and the *Nītiśāstra* alike there is much in common sense, and that is often in accord with practical

> morality; at no time can we regard the didactic fable as intended merely to extol cleverness without morality; there lingers around the work a distinct influence of the Dharmaśāstra, as only to be expected, seeing that the *Pañcatantra* was intended for the instruction of the young and the instructors were the brāhmaṇas.
>
> — quoted in Pathak, 1974: 19

In general, though, the fables of the Jātakas and the *Pañcatantra* fables are class apart in the ideology they seek to promote. The typical discourse of the *Pañcatantra* fables rests, as already said above, on their proximity with the conceptual utterances of Cāṇakya and Bhartṛhari in the form of the *gāthā*s contained in them. Though this is true of all the versions of the *Pañcatantra*, the thematic distinctiveness provided by the quotations from political and philosophical texts surfaces most in the *Hitopadeśa*:

> In *Hitopadeśa* interspersed throughout the fables are the maxims of wisdom and morality in verse . . . the maxims are drawn from various treatises on law and morality — from the Śatakas of Bhartṛhari, from Cāṇakya . . . similar to the maxims one comes across in Hebrew scriptures, in the proverbs of Solomon, in *Wisdom*, and in *Ecclesiasticus*.
>
> — Hale-Wortham, "Preface," *Hitopadeśa*, 1924: x

Critics, like Sternbach, have studied the relation between Cāṇakya verses and the *Hitopadeśa*. The influence of Cāṇakya verses is all-pervasive in the Indian literature:

> Cāṇakya verses have been borrowed from other collections, and they have been borrowed into other collections, so that there is not a general Sanskrit anthology of the past thousand years that entirely lacks them. — Ingalls, 1966: 2

Sternbach in his *Cāṇakya-Nīti-Text Tradition* mentions about 100 printed editions of one collection of Cāṇakya verses alone (Ingalls, 1966: 1). They are popular, because they suggest ways to benefit oneself without too much adherence to the difficult rules of ethics and morality, which has gone well with people. They are in fact remembered as proverbs, like folklore-proverbs.

Most of the Cāṇakya verses truly promulgate a Machiavellian attitude to life. What is important, according to him, is one's interest being fulfilled. It is not at all important whether the means employed are ethical or not. Some of the sayings are radically in the favour of profit and interest, without showing any botheration for the rules of ethics:

> Be not too straight, but look to the woods.
> Straight trees are cut but the crooked stand.
> — Sternbach, 1963: 63; Cāṇakya verse 6.5

A good number of fables in the *Hitopadeśa*, for instance, freely advocate the ideology of using crooked means for self-benefit or self-protection. The frame-narrative of Piṅgalaka and Sañjīvaka is a case in point. The foxes, Karataka and Damanaka, exploit a crooked strategy full of deceit and falsehood to get rid of the Bull in order to enjoy the benefit that the company of the Lion would bestow. In the story of the family of the Crow and the Serpent, the former uses a trick to get rid of his enemy. A small family of crow lived on a tree. In its trunk lived the Serpent, who would always devour the young crows. The Crow finally thought of a crooked means. Once, when the prince had come to bathe in the nearby pond, he picked up his gold chain and dropped it inside the tree trunk. The soldiers found the black Serpent inside the hollow of the tree, and killed him before obtaining the gold chain back. Likewise, in the frame-narrative of the third book, the most experienced minister suggests crooked means of deception to defeat a stronger enemy.

Thus, the fable delineates an important policy enshrined in the *nīti* discourse, which is the use of any means suitable for self-protection. We can quote a verse for its basic principle, the source of which goes back to the *Mahābhārata*:

> You should give up a man for a family,
> Give up a family for a village,
> Give up a village for a country,
> But sell out the world for yourself.
> — Sternbach, 1963: 63; Cāṇakya verse 1.7

It is this perception of self-protection and self-interest that contributes to the development of *rājanīti*. In Cāṇakya's terms, Damanaka would be an ideal minister that any king would like to have. The ability to devise great stratagems that he possesses is what is commended about a minister in the form of pithy sayings in the political discourse of the *Arthaśāstra*.

As discussed earlier, the various discourses proclaimed in the various knowledge-texts and used in the fable-narratives are also as much part of the folk. Hence, the animal narratives also reflect the folklore. While discussing the relations of the fables to the folklore, we might remember that though the study of folklore assumed importance in the form of ethnographic studies in the nineteenth century in the West, in India we have had a traditionally oral culture. The narrative literature has come down to us spoken by the lips of many anonymous story-tellers, which became a part of the folk. They closely observed the behaviours of men and women.

> The *Pañcatantra* gives us an adequate idea of the customs and manners, food habit, dresses, art and culture, and the beliefs and superstitions of the people of the contemporary Indian society. — Barthakuria, 1992: 3

We have already discussed that the work contains innumerable subjects like politics, religion, civil and criminal law, moral principles, and systems of education; it also adequately reflects the customs and manners of the age, and many other aspects of life. In this way, the *Pañcatantra* is an encyclopaedia of ancient Indian culture.

In fact, in reading the *Pañcatantra* or in reading any other Indian fable-composition, a reader has to perform many readings. The first time the reader would like to study the fable from the point of view of its contents, because the apparent form of the fable and the interest generated by the words and the behaviours of the animal characters would attract his/her attention. However, on a close reading, the second time, he/she might discover a perspective about the customs prevalent in the ancient India, inherent in the fable. It becomes important "to point out that the tales contained in the *Pañcatantra,* though fables, depict faithfully the common lives of the Indian people" (Sternbach, 1948: 86). The same is true about the Jātakas. A reader may discover layers of meanings, which are not only limited to the religious discourse, but also reflect simple lives and activities of the people.

> Thus they can be, and were probably meant to be read at a variety of levels, and function along lines of both common sense and Buddhist ethics, often welding the two together in complex, not always harmonious compositions.
>
> — Roy, 1996: 27

T.W. Rhys Davids, who pioneered the modern studies on Buddhism, argues that the Jātakas are "the oldest, most complete and most important collections of the folklore extant" ("Preface," *Buddhist Birth Stories*, vol. 1, 1880: iv). Though their importance depends as it were on the religious discourse contained in them and their depiction of the life and teaching of the Buddha, they have in them a mass of material that the folklorists consider extremely valuable. There are critics who even go to the extent of claiming that the Buddha used the popular stories and he infused the discursive content in them to give the form that they eventually acquired.

In other words, it is suggested that the Jātaka fables, in their content, are adaptations from the folklore:

> The Jātaka stories, though Buddhistic in form, are really adaptations of still more ancient tales current in the land between the Indus and the Ganges long before the rise of Buddhism.
> — Jackson, 1918: 280

For example, the fables like "Ass in the Lion Skin" and "The Fox and the Crow" that have been an integral part of the folk imagination for centuries have descended from the Jātakas.

The Jātaka fables make important statements about the historical awareness contained in the early Indian narratives. The stories highlight the pre-eminence of the Buddha and explain the Buddhist doctrines through narratives about the social life and customs of ancient India. The Jātakas are read today by historians as the sources of early Indian history (Roy, 1996: 23-40). The opening itself of each fable suggests an attempt to provide a solid social and historical reality. The Jātaka fable maintains an acute historical sense:

> Once upon a time, when Brahmadatta was reigning in Benares, the *bodhisattva* came to life as an ox, named Big Red, on the squire's estate in a certain hamlet. And he had a younger brother who was known as Little Red. There were only two brothers to do all the draught work of the family.
> — *The Jātaka*, 1990: 75

In all the narratives an elaborate setting is established, and though the exact historical identification is not possible, apart from the name Benares, the characters, their activities, beliefs and attitudes reflect a comprehensive view of the Indian society. This element of realism would have made the Jātaka fables so popular that they were represented through sculpture as early as the third century BCE. That is the reason why the contemporary historians have to depend on the Jātakas, and other Indian narratives, for the historical understanding of the ancient India.

> As such they have often been regarded as the closest approximation to the "popular" which we can hope to recover from the relatively remote past. — Roy, 1996: 23

Even the dissemination of the Buddhist messages was based on the need to take the Buddhist stories to the people at large. This position is associated with the Mahāyāna sect of Buddhism. In the first century CE, a new Buddhist sect arose, which called itself Mahāyāna, "the greater vehicle". This sect believed that the other Buddhist traditions placed too much emphasis on the attainment of *nīrvāṇa* as the primary goal of Buddhist spiritual practice. It is better instead, they contended, to emulate the Buddha's earlier experiences as a *bodhisattva*. In another major departure, the Mahāyāna began to use Sanskrit for a wider social reach of the Buddhist knowledge systems, including the fables contained in the Jātakas.

Thus, there was a radical ideology within Buddhism that worked for a greater connection between the Jātakas and the folk. The *Jātakamālā* is a by-product of this ideology. It was composed by Āryaśūra in Sanskrit, so as to take the Jātakas to those people who did not speak Prākṛt or Pāli. The *Jātakamālā* became an integral part of the folk, as shown by the inscriptions on the Ajantā frescos dating back to the sixth century CE. One of the reasons of its close connection with the folk was because it promoted, in the main, the Buddhist virtue of compassion, which had more social dimension than the other Buddhist virtues. There is a Tibetan tradition of reading one of the Jātaka narratives as the climax of the Great Prayer Festival celebrated during every Tibetan New Year. This is another indication of the proximity between the Jātaka and the folklore.

The same is the case with the *Mahābhārata*. The fables that were inserted in the epic, along with ballads and legends and other form of folk tales, in fact constituted the beliefs, customs and traditions of the common people. Every popular simile and analogy played an important role in the development of fables (Kawthekar, 1965: 123). During the expansion of the *Mahābhārata*, the fables that were included were from the popular narrative literature. So much replete with folk content are the fables of the epic that, because of the fables and other small non-fable popular narratives, it developed into an encyclopaedia of folklore:

> Even the famous sacrifice of serpents indicates inventive tendency of common people who express their beliefs, customs and traditions through primitive notions regarding their ancient associates as beasts and birds. — Kawthekar, 1965: 125

The popularity of the fables in the *Mahābhārata* can be understood from the fact that some of the fables in the epic have been expressed in contracted forms. They are not narrated in detail. It can be assumed with certainty that they were so much part of the folklore that there was no need felt to narrate them in detail:

> It means that the fables, remains of which are now preserved in the *Mahābhārata*, were so popular and known to the contemporary readers that the author did not think it necessary to elaborate it in full. — Kawthekar, 1965: 127

In one such case of an extremely contracted fable, Vidura asks Duryodhana to be friendly towards the Pāṇḍavas, and warns him that if he persisted in his inhuman treatment of them, the result would be dangerous. He quotes the example of the goat that digs a weapon out of the earth, and gets killed by it.

Very frequently, the epic resorts to analogies with the various abilities and habits demonstrated by the animals to suggest important thoughts. These brief analogies often become part of the language of the social exchange. In the "Śānti-Parva," for instance, on being asked by Yudhiṣṭhira about the various qualities of the combatants in the king's army, Bhīṣma says,

> It is proper that those weapons and vehicles should be adopted (by particular bodies of combatants) with which they have become familiar by use. Brave soldiers, adopting those weapons and vehicles, engage in battle. The *gandharvas*, the Sindhus, and the Sauvīras fight best with their nails and lances. They are brave and endued with great strength. Their armies are capable of vanquishing all forces; the Uśīnaras are possessed of great strength and skilled in all kinds of weapons. The Easterners are skilled in fighting from the backs of elephants and are conversant with all the ways of unfair fight. The Yavanas, the Kāmbojas, and those that dwell around Mathurā are well skilled in fighting with bare arms. The Southerners are skilled in fighting sword in hand. It is well known that persons possessed of great strength and great courage are born in almost every country. Listen to me as I describe their indications. They that have voices and eyes like those of the lion or the tiger, they that have a gait like that of the lion and the tiger, and they that have eyes like those of the pigeon or the snake, are all heroes capable of grinding hostile ranks. They that have a voice like deer, and eyes like those of the leopard or the bull, are possessed of great activity. They, whose voice resembles that of bells, are excitable, wicked, and wrathful. They that have a voice deep as that of the clouds that have wrathful face, or faces like those of camels, they that have hooked noses and tongues, are possessed of great speed and can shoot or hurl their weapons to a great distance. They that have bodies curved like that of the cat, and thin hair and thin skin, become endued with great speed and restlessness and almost invincible in battle. Some that

> are possessed of eyes closed like those of the iguana disposition that is mild, and speed and voice like the horses, are competent to fight all foes. They that are of well-knit and handsome and symmetrical frames, and broad chests, that become angry upon hearing the enemy's drum or trumpet, that take delight in affairs of every kind, that have eyes indicative of gravity, or eyes that seem to shoot out, or eyes that are green, they that have faces darkened with frowns, or eyes like those of the mongoose, are all brave and capable of casting away their lives in battle. They that have crooked eyes and broad foreheads and cheek-bones not covered with flesh and arms strong as thunderbolts and fingers bearing circular marks, and that are lean with arteries and nerves that are visible, rush with great speed when the collision of battle takes place. Resembling infuriated elephants, they become irresistible. — "Śānti Parvan", *The Mahābhārata*

These analogies with the animal lives appeal to popular imagination. It is not surprising, therefore, that in the later ages, expressions such as these became an integral part of the people's vocabulary in the form of proverbs.

Indeed, the folk customs and practices and popular religions contained in the fables throw light on ancient habits and beliefs. This is because the narrative has come to us directly from the people who lived at that stage of the human civilisation, unlike the "literary" tale or narrative, which exists only in the professed work of literature and is frozen therein.

> Just as knowledge is by and large constituted in the mind, it is also stored in the mind. This is another requirement of the oral culture. This requirement . . . has determined the style and structure of the texts. — Kapoor, 2005

The Indian fables, like other folk-genres, the myths, place and hero legends, drolls, *Marchens*, cumulative stories and ballads are narrated to and adopted from the folk.

The fables in the Jātakas and the *Mahābhārata* were part of the oral traditions first before they were put to writing, and even though those in the *Pañcatantra* and its various recensions were composed first (some critics think they came from the folk), they became subsequently the part of the folk, because they could be disseminated through oral means only. Thus, the fable sustained itself through the expression of mental sharing of the culture. The narrative in fact lives with the people.

There is a contention among those who have studied the Indian fables as to whether the fables have borrowed from the folklore or it is the other way round. Critics, like W. Norman Brown, go to the extent of claiming that themes suggested by the fables are present in the modern life. He makes a distinction between pure literature and oral forms, and argues that the lives depicted in the fables of those times, and the issues that the characters in the narratives confront, are still relevant to the Indian people. So the fables are to be found in the contemporary folk:

> The customs and superstitions portrayed in them are as a rule either those existing at the present or else pure myth, with the exception of those scattered instances where a literary story borrowed by the folk is still so fresh in the popular memory as to preserve the incidents of the times past when the story received its literary form. It can be said with truth, however, that there are many customs and beliefs of the folk appearing in the oral fiction that occur only rarely, if at all, in the literature. — Brown, 1919: 4-5

In India, the separation between a composition attributed to an author like Viṣṇu Śarmā and the folklore does not exist because of the frequent exchanges between the two. If it is true that the many narratives, in the remote past, had their origin and their existence among the folk, in the pre-literary times, and were later adopted into the compositions, it is equally true that many narratives existed in compositions first and then they were transferred to the folklore, and still continue to be the part of the modern Indian folklore.

> In other cases, stories have in all likelihood been carried by literary means to places where they did not exist previously, and have thus been implanted in the folklore.
>
> — Brown, 1919: 5-6

As an example of the borrowing of the folklore from the composed narrative, we can take the famous non-fable narrative, "The Magic Lamp" from Alexander Campbell's collection *Santhal Folk Tales*. It is a reworking of *Aladdin and the Wonderful Lamp*. Here, it is easier to confirm the borrowing of a folk tale from composed narrative, because the source narrative is not Indian.

We can establish the long connection between the Indian fables and the Indian folklore by discussing a particular fable that appears in the collection by W. Crooke from the then provinces of Agra and Oudh, *Talking Thrush*. This is known as a folk fable, but it has come down over centuries from the *Mahābhārata*. In the folklore, this fable is narrated by a brass founder, and it is entitled "The Camel's Neck." There is a camel that follows the most difficult austerities. The god is pleased and reveals himself to him. Seeing the god, the camel asks, "who are you?" "I am the Lord of the Three Regions," answers the god. "Show me your proper form," asks the camel. Then the god appears in his *caturbhujī* (four-handed) form, and the camel worships him. The god says he is happy with the camel, and so the animal can ask him a boon. "Let my neck be a *yojana* long," the camel requests. After having got such a long neck the lazy camel can now easily graze without moving his body. One day it rains, and so the beast puts his head and neck inside a cave to avoid getting wet. A pair of jackals also enters the cave. They see the attractive flesh of the *yojana*-long neck; they get tempted and begin eating it. The camel curls his head around to see what is annoying him but before he can get his neck back the jackals have eaten enough to kill him.

This fable is very popular not only in this region but also in other parts of India, with some variations of situation and character. It does appear as a creation of folk mind, but actually it has come straight from the *Mahābhārata*, Parva XII.112, which goes on to show the relationship between the fable and the folk in India. This fable appears there only with a few minor variations. It is said:

> In the Kṛta age there lived a camel that had recollection of all the acts of his former life. By observing vows and practising penances, he obtained favour with the puissant Brahmā, so that the god determined to grant him a boon. "Let my neck become long," asked the camel, "so that I may seize food even at the distance of a hundred *yojanas*." "Let it be so," said the god. The foolish animal became lazy and from that day on never went out grazing. One day while his neck was extended a hundred *yojanas*, a great storm arose. The camel placed his head and portion of his neck inside a cave to escape the storm. A pair of jackals also dragged themselves inside that very cave and entered it for shelter. The jackals began to eat the neck. The camel, when he perceived that his neck was being eaten, strove to shorten it; but as he moved it up and down, the jackals, without losing their hold upon it, continued to eat away. Within a short time, the camel died.

At the end of the fable, the narrator says:

> Thus did that foolish camel meet with his death then.
> Behold what a great evil followed in the train of idleness.
> — *The Mahābhārata*, Parva XII.112

The verse at the end of the folk tale reads:

> Idleness is a great fault: behold, what its fruit was;
> By it the foolish camel met with death, owing to his own deeds.
> — quoted in Brown, 1919: 8

Hence, we can see that there is a close proximity between these two versions, along with the verses that contain their discourse. Likewise, there are other examples of fables in the folklore that have directly come from the classical fable-compositions and vice versa.

In some cases, it is not the full narrative that is found in the folk, but only the incidents and motifs from the narratives. These are the story-units which are rearranged and given a different shape in the folklore, with the result that the folk narrative, as such, might be originally local, but its inputs might have come from the major compositions. The means by which the narratives are carried into the folklore vary. In some cases, the professional narrators, through the *kathāvācana* tradition, take the stories, especially from the *Mahābhārata* and the Jātaka, to different regions of India. It is a great tradition whereby the narrators travel village after village and give long recitations. They take pleasure in narrating them to the folk. Travelling merchants and the wandering *sādhus* are other people who are responsible for the dissemination of the stories among the folk. Another popular context is the narration in the family, especially by the grandparents.

Quite a large number of folk tales found in different regions of India today can be traced to the parallel tales and fables found in the Jātakas, the *Mahābhārata*, the *Pañcatantra*, the *Tantrākhyāyikā*, the versions contained in Somadeva's *Kathāsaritsāgara*, and Kṣemendra's *Bṛhatkathāmañjarī*, the Southern *Pañcatantra*, Pūrṇabhadra's *Pañcākhyānaka*, and the *Hitopadeśa*. W. Norman Brown in his *Pañcatantra in the Modern Indian Folklore* attempts a comprehensive analysis of the folk tales of India as far as their lineage is traced to the fables of the numerous versions of the *Pañcatantra*. He makes a table to show the links between the folk tales and fables of the classical compositions. The table sufficiently supports the claim that the folk tales have been derived from the fables of the classical compositions like the Jātakas, the *Mahābhārata*, the *Pañcatantra*, etc.

We can take the frame-narrative from the first book of the *Pañcatantra* and delineate the relationship between the folk tale and the classical fable. The narrative of the Lion and the Bull is traced centuries later in the *Fables and Folk Tales From an Eastern Forest* collected by Walter Skeat and in the *Village Folk Tales of Ceylon* collected and translated by H. Parker, with little variations. In the narrative collected by Parker, the Jackal meets the friendly pair of the Lion and the Bull. He observes their friendship and expresses to the Bull his wish to be accepted as friends. The Bull refuses, and in order to avenge himself upon it, he intrigues a situation to force a quarrel between the two friends. He instigates the Lion by telling him that the Bull desires to be more powerful and, in the process, dominate him. On the other hand, he traps the Bull by telling him that the Lion wants to kill him with his roar. Deceived by the Jackal, the two friends fight. While the Lion's roar kills the bull, the Bull gores the Lion to death.

A comparison of the *Pañcatantra* fable with its folk versions shows a good deal of innovation on the part of the folklorist. In the *Pañcatantra*, there are two jackals/foxes, Karataka and Damanaka instead of one, and they are already known to the Lion, as they are the sons of one of his former ministers. They in fact bring the Bull, Sañjīvaka to the Lion, as here it is the latter who is scared of the roar of the Bull. The foxes decide to intrigue the moment they see the Bull. Damanaka says as he approaches Sañjīvaka:

> Oh! this is just as well. Making a pact between him and the king and later enmity between them, would bring Piṅgalaka under my influence. — *The Pañcatantra*, 2006: 49

The Lion and the Bull become great friends. They become so attached as friends that the Lion ignores the foxes and his other subjects completely. Karataka and Damanaka intrigue to separate the two friends by instilling distrust and anger in the Lion for the Bull, as a result of which the two friends fight, and the Lion kills the Bull.

The folk tale is different from the *Pañcatantra* fable in the sense that the Lion and the Bull are already friends before the Jackal appears on the scene, and secondly, both the Lion and the Bull are killed in the fight. Now, this fable has been traced to the Tibetan Jātakas as the ultimate origin. Norman Brown contends that it is unlikely that the fables found in the Tibetan Jātakas were derived from the Indian folklore. It is highly possible, he says, that the fable was originally conceived in the Jātakas; from there it entered into the *Pañcatantra,* and then it was adopted into the folklore. Whether actually the fable is derived from the Jātakas or the *Pañcatantra,* or vice versa is a matter of debate, but the fact that there exists a close relation between the Indian fable and the Indian folklore is established beyond point.

3

Indian Fables
A Study in Form and Structure

> Bowing to the Buddha as he sat cross-legged there, the Brethren too seated themselves around him. Then they asked him saying, "Only the present is known to us, sir; the past is hidden from us. Make it known to us." And at their request, he told this story of the past. — *Vattaka Jātaka*

THE fable is only one of the numerous small narrative genres used by writers the world over. However, it is considered the most effective genre to point out a moral or a discourse. This chapter argues that for the fable to become an effective discursive tool its narrative form is equally responsible. Hence, if the Indian fables constitute a corpus of serious knowledge, the narrative form responsible for the expression of this knowledge is also important to consider. In fact, the greater interest in their content, generated by the fables over the centuries, has been greatly for the form that they take. That they delineate the moral discourse of the Buddha or the political principles of Cāṇakya or Bhīṣma has not only been the factor for their renown. The listener or the reader is instantly struck by the naïvety of the form and the structure of the narratives. It is a unique quality of the Indian fables that combines, through the formal features, amusement, and serious discourses.

The *Pañcatantra* became popular not only for the fact that the narratives expressed issues discussed in Cāṇakya's

Arthaśāstra and Bharata's *Nāṭyaśāstra*, but also for the fact that it were the Crow and the Donkey who could utter the philosophy of these thinkers. It is not only the fact that the *bodhisattva* preaches *dhamma*, which instantly arrests the reader's interests, but that he takes the form of the Quail and the Fish to do so makes the stories even more interesting. Scholars and critics of the Indian fable have found impressive not only the comprehensive Indian discourses encapsulated in the narratives but also the manner in which they have been told, making the whole process a novel invention.

> We may say without exaggeration that we owe to India not only the idea whereby moral and spiritual truth is conveyed under concrete forms, but also some of those very identical forms under which this truth was originally conveyed to the Eastern peoples
>
> — Wortham, "Preface," *Hitopadeśa*, 1924: viii

The Indian fable has not only been a novel contribution to the world literature from a historical perspective, it has, actually, also inspired formal and structural innovations in literature. While writers of different narrative genres have through ages modelled their narratives on certain principles of narrative construction found in the fables, some formal features of the Indian fable also seem contemporary. Some such formal features are the cohesion of narrative and discursive elements within a story, the use of frame-story as a discursive and narrative strategy, the use of both prose and poetic forms within the same narrative, contracted narratives, and the use of aphorisms. Above all, the intertextuality of the stories is very remarkably modern.

The *Mahābhārata* introduces one major innovation in the fable-genre, and this innovation suggests the variety of ways into which the fable-form can be exploited to communicate a discourse. It is to the *Mahābhārata* that we owe the flexibility of the fable-form. The fable is primarily a metaphorical statement, and it is not limited to a fixed form or length. In the epic, we find fables ranging from a number of pages to even a single sentence. Between these two extremes lie the contracted fables — of, say, a paragraph. For instance, in "Śānti-Parva," we get an apt example of contracted fable. Karṇa has been killed by Arjuna. Yudhiṣṭhira and other Pāṇḍavas are grieving as they have known that Karṇa was the eldest of the Pāṇḍavas. Dharmarāja, Yudhiṣṭhira, is contemplating retirement to the forest to perform a penance. In this situation, Arjuna tries to lift the spirits of the Pāṇḍavas by telling a discourse, which includes a contracted fable. This discourse, including the fable, subsequently became popular as a universal philosophical truth:

> Only a few men that are of noble disposition adore in all their acts those among the gods that are equally disposed towards all creatures and that are self-restrained and peaceful. I do not behold the creature in this world that supports life without doing any act of injury to others. Animals live upon animals, the stronger upon the weaker. The mongoose devours mice; the cat devours the mongoose; the dog devours the cat; the dog again is devoured by the spotted leopard. Behold all things again are devoured by the Destroyer when he comes! This mobile and immobile universe is food for living creatures. This has been ordained by the gods. The man of knowledge, therefore, is never stupefied at it. It behoveth thee, O great king, to become that which thou art by birth. Foolish (kṣatriyas) alone, restraining wrath and joy take refuge in the woods. The very ascetics cannot support their lives without killing creatures.
>
> — *The Mahābhārata*, Śānti-Parva

This contracted fable presents a universal reality and refers to a bitter truth perceived in the world. This is a perfect example of the fable being integrated in the larger narrative framework of the epic. The brevity of the fable-form, the form of the contracted fable, adds to the force of Arjuna's argument that the Pāṇḍavas should stoically view the death of Karṇa.

The most remarkable use of fables to be found in the *Mahābhārata* suggests further precision of thought and expression. The one-line fables occur quite prominently in the text as a part of the figurative language, and they are again closely related to the overall discourse of the situation they are part of. The most perfect way to talk about the one-line fable in the *Mahābhārata* would be to quote a series of such fables that occur in the conversation between Śalya and Karṇa in "Karṇa-Parva." Śalya speaks to Karṇa, and tries to pacify the latter's pride:

> In desiring, O Karṇa, to fight today with Arjuna of keen-edged feats, thou art for rubbing all thy limbs against the keen edges of a trident. This thy challenge of Arjuna, O Sūta's son, is like that of a foolish young little deer of activity challenging a huge lion excited with wrath. Do not, O Sūta's son, challenge that prince of mighty energy like a fox gratified with meat in the forest challenging the maned monarch of the forest. Do not be destroyed, encountering Arjuna. Thou, O Karṇa, challengest Dhanañjaya, the son of Pṛthā, even like a hare challenging a mighty elephant with tusks large as plough-shafts, and with the juice issuing out of its mouth and rent cheeks. From folly thou art piercing, with a piece of wood, the black cobra of virulent poison excited to fury within its hole, in desiring to fight with Pārtha. Endued with little understanding, thou, O Karṇa, disregarding that lion among men, viz. the son of Pāṇḍu, yellest at him, like a jackal that, disregarding a maned lion excited with wrath, yells at him. As a snake, for its own destruction, challenges that foremost of birds, viz. Vinatā's son, possessed of beautiful plumage and great activity, even so dost thou, O Karṇa, challenge Dhanañjaya the son of

> Pāṇḍu. Thou desirest to cross without a raft the terrible ocean, the receptacle of all the waters, with its mountain waves and teeming with aquatic animals, when at its height at the rise of the Moon. O Karṇa, thou challengest Dhanañjaya, the son of Pṛthā, to battle even like a calf challenging a smiting bull of keen horns and neck thick as a drum. Like a frog croaking at a terrible and mighty cloud yielding copious showers of rain, thou croakest at Arjuna who is even like Parjanya among men. As a dog from within the precincts of the house of his master barks at a forest-roaming tiger, even so, O Karṇa, thou barkest at Dhanañjaya, that tiger among men. A jackal, O Karṇa, residing in the forest in the midst of hares regardeth himself a lion till he actually sees a lion. Even so, O son of Rādhā, thou regardest thyself a lion, for thou dost not behold that repressor of foes, that tiger among men, viz. Dhanañjaya. Thou regardest thyself a lion till thou beholdest the two Kṛṣṇas stationed on the same car like Sūrya and Candramā. As long as thou dost not hear the twang of *gāṇḍīva* in great battle, so long art thou able to do what thou pleasest. Beholding Pārtha, causing the ten points of the compass to resound with the roar of his car and the twang of his bow, and beholding him roaring like a tiger, thou wilt become a jackal. Thou art always a jackal, and Dhanañjaya always a lion. O fool, in consequence of thy envy and hatred for heroes, thou always, seemest to be like a jackal. As a mouse and a cat are to each other in strength, or a dog and a tiger, a fox and a lion, or a hare and an elephant, as falsehood and truth, as poison and nectar, even so art thou and Pārtha known to all by your respective deeds.
>
> — *The Mahābhārata*, Karṇa-Parva

This would be one of the most remarkable instances in world literature of the interwoven series of one-line fable-narrative.

As must be evident from the above example, the fables in the Indian texts are contained within another, a larger narrative framework, which is called the frame-narrative. The fables are all set within the frame-narratives, invented for the first time in the Indian fable-compositions. The fables of the *Pañcatantra*, for example, are an inter-woven series of narratives set within five frame-narratives, but, apart from them, the beginning of the work itself is a frame-narrative for the whole text, the narrative about the King Anantaśakti and the dull princes and Viṣṇu Śarmā. In each of the five books of the *Pañcatantra*, there is a frame-story, whose line of progress is very often disturbed by a host of other stories. We often find a narrative originating within another, and forming many layers sometimes, which close unexpectedly, and again take the reader back to the frame-narrative.

The Jātaka fables about the *bodhisattva*'s experiences are also set within the frame-story involving the Buddha and his disciples. In the *Mahābhārata*, the fables have been set within the epic proper. The characters choose to narrate fables at different critical points in the epic action, so naturally the fables are set within the larger narrative framework of the epic. However, the structure of the frame-narrative is unique in the case of each of these fable-compositions, because the philosophy, nature, and overall structure of the compositions of which the fables are a part are different. In the *Mahābhārata*, the frame-narrative shapes up in this manner:

> Janamejaya said, "When that tiger among men, of righteous soul and great energy, firmly adhering to truth and with passions under complete control, viz. the son of Śāntanu and Gaṅgā, named Devavrata or Bhīṣma of unfading glory, lay on a hero's bed with the sons of Pāṇḍu sitting around him, tell me, O great sage, what converse ensued in that meeting of heroes after the slaughter of the troops."
>
> Vaiśampāyana said, "When Bhīṣma that chief of the Kurus, lay on his bed of arrows, many *ṛṣis* and *siddhas*, O king, headed by Nārada, came to that spot. The unslain remnant

> of the (assembled) kings with Yudhiṣṭhira at their head, and Dhṛtarāṣṭra and Kṛṣṇa and Bhīma and Arjuna and the twins also came there. Those high-souled persons, approaching the grandsire of the Bharatas who looked like the Sun himself dropped from the firmament, indulged in lamentations for him. Then Nārada of godlike features reflecting for a short while, addressed all the Pāṇḍavas and the unslain remnant of the kings saying, 'The time, I think, has come for you to question Bhīṣma (on subject of morality and religion), for Gaṅgā's son is about to expire like the Sun that is on the point of setting. He is about to cast off his life-breaths. Do you all, therefore, solicit him to discourse to you? He is acquainted with the varied duties of all the four orders. Old in years, after abandoning his body he will obtain high regions of bliss. Solicit him, therefore, without delay, to clear the doubts that exist in your minds.'" Thus addressed by Nārada. . . .
>
> — The *Mahābhārata,* Karṇa-Parva

It is while answering the various questions on ethics, morality and polity posed by mainly Yudhiṣṭhira that Bhīṣma exploits the fable-form. This frame-narrative contains the fables as a fruit contains kernels, so is the case with the frame-narratives in the Jātaka and the *Pañcatantra.* The same is the way in which the fables are framed in the other *parvas* of the *Mahābhārata.*

So, technically speaking, a frame-story is a narrative method whereby a main narrative framework is composed so as to organise a set of stories within. Each of these stories is a story within a story. For example, in the first book of the *Pañcatantra,* "Mitrabheda," the reader comes across the frame-narrative about the friendship between Piṅgalaka and Sañjīvaka, the Lion and the Bull, and about the breaking up of their friendship, the fight between the two, and the killing of the Bull, all because of a trick played by the fox-brothers, Karataka and Damanaka. Within this frame-narrative, there are framed 23 narratives, 10 narrated by Damanaka and eight by his brother Karataka. There are three more stories intercalated even further within the fables narrated by the two foxes. The three of these stories are narrated by the Sparrow, Tiṭibhi, one by the Jackal and the magistrate each. So, we have the case of a series of a story within a story that suggests how intricate the plot of the *Pañcatantra* becomes.

All the 547 narratives of the Jātakas are set within the frame-narrative of the Buddha and his disciples, whereas in the *Mahābhārata* there are various characters like Bhīṣma or Vidura who become the part of the frame within which the fables are set. The frame-narrative form has been subsequently used in many of the larger Indian narrative literatures other than the *Mahābhārata*. These larger texts have used both fable and non-fable narratives inside their main narrative framework. One of the most prominent among such texts are the *Rāmāyaṇa*, the other being *Betāl Pacīsī*.

Now, in a way the Jātaka, the *Mahābhārata* and the *Pañcatantra* initiated a kind of frame-narrative tradition, with authors throughout the world, till today, emulating this method invented by the Buddha and Viṣṇu Śarmā. This form reached Europe chiefly by ways of trade routes, as the Arabs migrated to Spain, Sicily, and Constantinople; they were also carried by the returning armies from the crusades. It spread and became popular throughout the world because of its inherent structure and flexibility. These different imitations in the distant cultures truly suggest the universality of the Indian frame-narrative form, which was meant to be used originally for the fables. Its influence outside India was to be found in the Arab world in the famous *Arabian Nights* (*The Book of One Thousand and One Nights*). Now, while the people in different parts of the world used the frame-narrative, they also modified the form to make it specific to their cultures. In the *Arabian Nights*, for instance, the frame-narrative has

Scheherazade narrating the fairy tales to the Shahryar. Like the *Pañcatantra*, many of the stories narrated by Scheherazade themselves futher become frames for other narratives, as for instance the stories narrated by Sindbād, the seaman, to Sindbād, the landsman.

B.E. Perry in his book, *The Origin of the Book of Sindbad*, talks about the parallels between the introduction to the *Pañcatantra* and the *Book of Sindbad*. He starts a debate here that continued for some time. He contends that the introduction and the frame-narrative of the former is in fact modelled on the latter composition. However, he himself contradicts his position by saying that the Arabic work is Pahlavī in origin. Dawood Ibrahim, on the other hand, in his article, "The Arab Frame Tradition," argues that

> it is a well-known fact that the Arabs learned the framing device from the Indians through the intermediary of the Persians and transmitted it to the West through a flux of important oriental narratives . . . that the framing device originated in India was recognised by scholars writing as early as in the nineteenth century, such as the Indologist Loiseleur Deslongchamps. — Ibrahim, 1984: 109

This seems true because all the major scholars of the Indian literature like S.K. De have established beyond doubt that the *Pañcatantra* was framed in its orignal Sanskrit version in its earliest stages (De, 1962: 86).

Ovid exploited this form in his *Metamorphosis*. Some of the other famous examples are: Boccacio's *Decameron*, where a group of young aristocrats, while escaping to the countryside to evade the plague, pass their times telling stories; Chaucer's the *Canterbury Tales*, in which a group of 29 pilgrims on a pilgrimage to the shrine of Thomas Beckett in Canterbury narrate stories to and from the journey; and Mary Shelley's novel *Frankenstein*, in which the character Robert Walton writes letters to his sister, in which he tells the stories in turn told to him by Victor Frankenstein.

There is interspersed another tale in the last text, which is twice removed from the frame-narrative; it is the story narrated by the monster to Victor about his unwholesome experiences. One of the most famous British employment of the frame-narrative is to be found in Emily Bronte's *Wuthering Heights*, which uses the frame story of Lockwood in order to narrate the story of Heathcliff and Catherine. Decameron also makes the frame-narrative the background of his work. The plague, for instance, stands for the demoralising pain and sorrows of life that the characters have left behind.

Therefore, literatures around the world have inherited from the Indian fables a method of story-telling, unique in its own way. More recently, the form has been used as a cinematic technique in Wojciech Jerzy Has's unusual and influential 1965 Polish film *The Saragossa Manuscript*.

However, the earliest example of the Western frame-narrative that we know today is *Westcar Papyrus*, an Egyptian narrative. This narrative is extant in a damaged condition, though it is sufficiently complete for the reader to get an idea of its form. In the frame-narrative, the sons of King Khufu or Cheops narrate each a story of magic, and the narrative goes on till that point when one of the sons frantically screams that there actually lives a real magician who surpasses all the characters they have talked about in their tales. Subsequently, this real magician is summoned, and he demonstrates the magic tricks in front of the royal audience.

> *Papyrus* belongs possibly to an age when the delineation of character was unkown to literary art. But in India, the collection of box tales were far more finished in execution.
>
> — Hinckley, 1934: 70

As far as the Indian fables are concerned, the frame-narrative primarily functions as a device to combine the narrative and discursive sections of the stories. In fact, a reader can easily break each fable into a narrative and a discursive text, by following the way a fable is set within a frame-story. In the Jātakas, the reader comes across four levels of narration. The *Lakkhana Jātaka* (No. 11) can be taken as an example. At the first level, an unnamed narrator, one of the Buddha's disciples, only simply identifies the story: "The Upright man." — This story was told by the Master in the Bamboogrove near Rājagaha about Devadatta. At the second level of narration, the Buddha and his disciples are shown as confronting a problem, again being narrated by the same unnamed narrator:

> For on the occasion now in question, Devadatta, through failing to carry the Five Points which he had pressed for, had made a schism in the Brotherhood and had gone off with 500 Brethren to dwell at Gayā-sisa. Now, these Brethren came to a riper knowledge; and the Master knowing this called the two chief disciples. . . .

At the third level of narration, the Buddha takes on the role of the narrator. It is at this level that the fable-narrative makes a transition from the human world to the animal world, in order to teach a point or moral:

> This is not the only time, Brethren, when glory has been Sāriputta's on his return with a following of his kinsfolk; like glory was his too in bygone days. So too this is not the only time when Devadatta has lost his following; he lost it also in bygone days.
>
> The Brethren asked the Blessed One to explain this to them. The Blessed One made clear what had been concealed by re-birth.

These three levels of narration are integrated into the fourth level of narration, which functions more importantly as a proclamation of the Buddhist discourse . . . in this fable it is about the qualities of a true leader. The fable, at the third level of narration, presents the *bodhisattva* as the chief of a herd of stags. He has his two sons, Luckie and Blackie, given the responsibilities of 500 stags, to be taken with safety to the forest, during the harvest season, when the villagers are on the lookout for the deer. With his wisdom and agility of mind, Luckie displays the ideal leadership, by protecting every single member of his herd, whereas the foolish Blackie loses all the members of his herd. The discursive conclusion which relates directly the frame-narrative, as uttered by the *bodhisattva* forms the fourth level of narration:

> The upright kindly man hath his reward
> Mark Luckie leading back his troop of kin,
> While here comes Blackie shorn of all his herd.
> — *The Jātaka*, 1990: 74-75

In the fifth and the final level of narration, the unnamed narrator again comes into the picture to describe the atmosphere around the Buddha, once this tale is finished, and then the characters are identified in their present life.

The interweaving of the narratives runs till one more level in the *Pañcatantra*, as compared to the Jātakas. In this book of fables, as in the Jātakas, we have an unnamed narrator in the first phase of the narrative. This narrator, whose identity is as anonymous as the unnamed Buddhist disciple, the first narrator in the Jātakas, relates the larger framework of the composition, story of the King Anantaśakti and his idiot sons. He narrates the entry of Viṣṇu Śarmā, the author-narrator (like the Buddha in the Jātakas) in the overall plot of the work. He is the one who introduces him in the text:

> He said, "Here we have in a group of wise sages a brāhmaṇa Viṣṇu Śarmā who is an authority in all Śāstras and popular

> among students. Hand over your children to him. He shall certainly make them intelligent.
>
> The king on listening to this, called Viṣṇu Śarmā, and said, "Bhagavān! Have grace upon me and teach my children *Arthaśāstra*, and make them extraordinarily wise. In return, I shall give you a hundred villages."
>
> — *The Pañcatantra*, 2006: 14

And hence, the narrative goes on narrated by this unnamed narrator till Viṣṇu Śarmā declares that he would compose the *Pañcatantra*, and use it as his pedagogical text, and his teaching methodolgy would be the narration of the stories, with specific discursive content, to the princes. From here, Viṣṇu Śarmā becomes our principal narrator. This can be called the second phase of narration in the *Pañcatantra*.

Viṣṇu Śarmā narrates the frame-narratives entirely. But, he offers the responsibility of narrating further stories to the principal characters, who figure in the frame-narratives. For instance, in the frame-narrative of the first book, the two fox-brothers take on the mantle of narration. What is remarkable to note during this phase of narration is the development of a dramatic situation that leads to the telling of each new narrative, which could actually be compared with the situation that the Jātaka fable presents while showing the Buddha and his disciples a little before the former begins to narrate his story. For example, the situation just before the first tale is narrated is extremely dramatic, as narrated by Viṣṇu Śarmā:

> Karataka replied: "Brother, why should we bother? What is the use of our thinking on this subject?"
>
> A person engaging in futile tasks not of his concern gets destroyed the same way as this monkey died a painful death upon drawing out a nail from the wood.

> Damanaka asks, "what is that tale?" Karataka narrated thus:
>
> — *The Pañcatantra*, 2006: 32-33

This makes up the third phase of narration. Now, the stories narrated by the characters within the frame-narrative would become the fourth phase of narration, and like the Jātakas, during the fifth phase of narration, the story stops the progress of events in order to directly communicate a discourse, as in the fifth story of the fourth book, "Labdhapraṇāśam." This story is about two lion cubs and a young jackal brought up together by a compassionate lioness and her husband. When the three young animals move out in the jungle, the young jackal gets scared seeing animals, which seems surprising to the lion cubs, because of their different races. The following discourse is expressed, which, though tied with the main narrative, forms a different level of narration, as it lifts itself from the immediate narrative context and connects to the human world.

> In a fight the enthusiasm of even one soldier encourages all and depression of one depresses all. Therefore, kings prefer strong, brave and steady-minded enthusiastic fighters and abandon cowards. — *The Pañcatantra*, 2006: 287-88

So, the lioness asks the young jackal to leave her family and join his own race, as his natural timidity might negatively impact her own children.

There are two more phases in the narration of the *Pañcatantra*, that make the text differently arranged than the Jātakas. One further step that the *Pañcatantra* goes in the engrafting of the narratives is when it makes the characters in the stories narrated by the characters in the frame-stories narrated by the principal narrator narrate another story. This is the fifth phase of narrative development in the *Pañcatantra*. For instance, the 12th narrative of the first book of the

Pañcatantra is about a pair of sparrows, Tiṭibha and Tiṭibhi; the 13th tale is narrated by Tiṭibhi, which is about the Tortoise and his swan friends. And for the sixth and the final phase of narration, the narrative comes back again to the frame-narrative, after such a long development.

In the *Hitopadeśa*, there is another development, which makes the text move up to another phase of narrativity, which is not there in its source book, the *Pañcatantra*. The narrative method employed by the text makes even the princes, who are silent listeners in the *Pañcatantra*, actively participate in the telling of the narratives. After the end of each book, the princes add their own understanding of the frame-story and the stories narrated within it, and, in their statements, there is a reiteration of the central discourse contained in the entire book. This makes up for another level of narration achieved in the *Hitopadeśa*. For instance, at the end of the second book of the work, "Suhṛdbheda" (Separation of Friends), the text has this:

> "Such," said Viṣṇu Śarmā to the princes, "is the "Separation of Friends"."
>
> The princes answered, "we have indeed been gratified."
>
> "Before we conclude," continued Viṣṇuśarmā, "this must be added:
>
> May the quarrels between friends exist only in the abodes of your enemies;
>
> May the traitors, as days go by, approach their destruction nearer and nearer;
>
> May happiness and prosperity ever dwell among the men of our land;
>
> And may boys of aftertime rejoice in the garden of fable."
>
> — *The Hitopadeśa*, 1924

On the basis of these different phases of the narrative processes employed in the two texts, a reader can structurally classify the stories contained in the Jātakas and the *Pañcatantra* into different units. But, the question is, what is responsible for the inter-linking or cohesiveness of the different units that make up the fable composition? There are primaily two factors that unite the different strands of the fable-composition: the narrator and the discourse. Before taking up the role of these two factors in giving a shape to the narratives, it is important to note the basic difference between the structure of the Jātakas and the *Pañcatantra*. Though these two factors of narrative unity act in more or less identical ways in these two fable-compositions, it is important to consider that, in the context of the Jātakas, by unity is meant the integration of the various narrative units of a single fable-narrative, whearas in the *Pañcatantra* it is that of an entire book.

The fables in the *Pañcatantra* construct a complete book, which suggests an erudite plot sense. The frame-narratives of each book do not simply perform the role of extending the occasions for narrating fables in a mechanical way. There is no perfunctory repetition of situations in the frame-narratives. Thus, an entire book of the *Pañcatantra* is structured quite efficiently. In the Jātakas, however, we get individual independent texts compiled together as a collection of different narrative utterances of the Buddha on different occasions. Hence, the various narrative units of the Jātakas form a pattern within a single fable, whearas in the case of the *Pañcatantra*, the complete pattern is formed by seeing a complete book as a text. The various units of the fables in the Jātakas that delineate a structural pattern are:

(a) Identification of the narrative,

(b) The frame-narrative,

(c) The story within the frame-narrative,

(d) The discourse in the verse form,

(e) Critical commentary on the verse, and

(f) Return to the frame-narrative.

A complete pattern builds up for an entire book in the *Pañcatantra*:

(a) The frame-narrative,

(b) The narrative contexts of each narrative,

(c) The story within the frame-narrative,

(d) The narrative verse,

(e) References to discursive texts,

(f) Intercalation of further narratives, and

(g) Going back to the frame-narrative.

Thus, every single narrative is an individual unit in the Jātakas, whereas in the *Pañcatantra*, every book is a whole unit.

All these narrative units of the Indian fables are connected by a single line of thought. In other words, there is a central discourse immanent in all these narrative units which keeps them together as clogs to a wheel. Indeed, the discourse delimits the structure of the Indian fables. In the *Pañcatantra*, each book posits a distinct political philosophy, and it is this that maintains the equivalence between the form and the content of the fable-narratives. It is the different kinds of characters, the diversity of ideologies expressed by them, and the constant negotiation between the narrative and discourse that make the *Pañcatantra* a densely textured and layered text.

Likewise, in the Jātakas, *paccuppannavatthu* (story of the present time), *atītavatthu* (the story of the past), *gāthā*s (the stanzas), *sambodhana* (identification of the personages in the "story of the past") are all connected by the central discourse. Essentially, each and every Jātaka narrative is an exposition of a specific Buddhist doctrine. But this is not as simple, but a complex arrangement, which also includes a heightened sense of time. What is meant is that time, discourse, and narrative, these three associate to build up the structure of an Indian fable. Each of these three, however, has meaning in a text with respect to the other two. To discuss the time first, it plays an important function in any narrative, and more so in the Indian fable-narrative.

In fact, it is the sense of time that brings the narrative and discourse closer in the Indian fables. In the Indian narratives, including the fables, universal time is an important concept. In the Jātaka fables, time integrates the Buddhist discourse with the narrative that the Buddha spins. Time not only combines the discourse and the narrative but also implicates the reader in the narrative-discourse. In *Vattaka-Jātaka* (No. 35), we find direct statements about the conceptualisation of time and its role in the narrative:

> Bowing to the Buddha as he sat cross-legged there, the Brethren too seated themselves around him. Then they asked him saying, "Only the present is known to us, sir; the past is hidden from us. Make it known to us." And at their request, he told this story of the past. . . .
>
> . . . "Thus, Brethren," said the Master, "it is not my present power but the efficacy of an Act of truth performed by me when a young quail, that has made the flames pass over this spot in the jungle." — *The Jātaka*, 1990: 89-90

Evidently, this fable foregrounds the Buddhist doctrine of Truthfulness, which exists in a temporal framework much larger than the perceptive powers of the characters in the frame-narrative. The act of truthfulness that took place in the past is not known to them, they don't have that divine vision, which the Buddha is gifted with, to see and realise it. So, this narrative makes an interesting distinction between real time and narrative time. The discourse exists in the narrative time, its full implication cannot be understood unless the Buddha's disciples could see the entire span of the narrative time, and hence the Buddha relates to them the narrative of the past and then connects it to the present time, for the characters and the readers to make sense of. In this way, time is a very important factor in the Jātakas.

In the way that the Buddha, as a narrator, connects the past with the present, in an effort to delimit the universal time to the span of real time, he also connects the present to the past, so as to reveal that every single event is happening within that vast span of time which contains the discourse of Truthfulness. In *Vānarinda Jātaka* (No. 57), for instance, the Buddha narrates the tale of the Crocodile who wanted to kill the Monkey in order to feed his heart to his wife. After finishing the tale, the narrator, Buddha, says,

> "This is not the first time then, Brethren, that Devadatta has gone about seeking to kill me; he did just the same in bygone days." And having ended his lesson, the Master showed the connection and identified the Birth by saying, "Devadatta was the crocodile of those days, the brāhmaṇa-girl Ciñcā was the Crocodile's wife, and I myself the Monkey-king." — *The Jātaka*, 1990: 143

Hence, clearly the overall narrative structure of the fable is governed by shifting time from present to past and back to present, and it is time that determines the connection between the narrative and the message.

So exactly is the case with the *Pañcatantra*. Time, as a constructive element inherent in the narratives, shifts constantly. There are direct references to different time periods, as said by the narrator in the 15th story of the third book:

> . . . that was the situation in *Satyayuga* because in that age even speaking to sinners brought sin. Therefore talking to the eagle caused the cloths to fall. This is *Kaliyuga*. In this age all men (creatures) are sinners by nature. Hence, without doing a sinful act, no sin attaches.
>
> — *The Pañcatantra*, 2006: 243-44

The narrative, in the *Pañcatantra*, would suddenly shift in time. The reference to the time would, as in the Jātakas, connect the narrative to its central discourse. Apart from the direct references to time, different temporal frameworks are suggested by the use of allusions. And this method is more effective in foregrounding the discourse that the narrative intends to convey. For instance, in a single narrative of the second book, we come across the following diverse observations:

(a) Why didn't Rāvaṇa consider kidnapping another's wife as wrong? Why, in the first place, Rāma didn't consider the impossibility of a golden deer? Even Yudhiṣṭhira agreed to play the game of dice only to win extermination from the land.

(b) A lion killed the proto-Grammarian Pāṇini; an elephant killed Sage Jaimini, a renowned seer and creator of the treatise on Logic (Mīmāṁsā); the alligator killed the master of stanzaic composition Piñjala.

(c) Cāṇakya opined one must do good deeds; Śaṅkarācārya said one must seek more and more friends; and Bṛhaspati taught the policy of not trusting another. — *Pañcatantra*, 2006: 151-59

There are many more such instances in the text. What is important to note is that all these references in the text mean to establish a certain kind of discourse, and, thereby, make the narrative extremely flexible in terms of time. Even more comprehensively than the Jātakas, the *Pañcatantra* fables convey the sense of universal time. The narrative is free to take recourse to any temporal framework to put across the discursive thought. Even in the allusion quoted above, all refer to specific time periods in the Indian history, and so, in a way, liberate the narrative from the constraint of temporal delimitation. But all serve to centralise a single line of thought, a common discourse.

In the context of the temporal axis that combines narrative with discourse, the role of the narrator becomes very crucial in the Indian fables. The narrator is the link between the text and the reader. Viṣṇu Śarmā is, in a way, the most avid listener in the text. He is the one who listens to the narration of all the different narrators in the text, and also the one who understands the various temporal and discursive shifts in the narratives. Hence, in a way the narrator serves as a crucial linking device to combine the different sections of the narratives. Likewise, the Buddha, as a narrator, keeps the temporal shifts from present to the past and back to the present compact as a unit, because he is the one who has experienced all the diverse temporal events. He is the one who mediates between the narrative and the reader. The Buddha integrates the narrative and links the characters and the situations of the present and the past. In fact, there are different ways adopted in the fables to reduce the infinite time to a limited time and space to suit the understanding of the readers. Hence, the narrative of the past is given a specific time and setting, which actually is imaginary and beyond any particular time and place:

> Once upon a time when Brahmadatta was in Benares the *bodhisattva* was born a deer and dwelt in the forest as the head of a herd of deer. — *The Jātaka*, 1990: 46

There relationship between the frame-narrative and the narrative within it, in the Jātakas, can indeed be seen in different ways. The story of the present is located in a different time and space than the story of the past. In fact, this temporal shift from present to past and back to present can be seen as an important narrative strategy employed to disseminate the Buddhist discourse:

> The relatively secular space envisaged in the story of the past probably permitted the lay audience to identify more closely with the proceedings. At the same time, the fact that access to this space was regulated through the framing story would have coloured the perceptions of it as well. — Roy, 1996: 26

The frame story of the present, however, is limited by time and space, which is distinctively religious. The narrative context of the Master and the disciples is placed in the religious atmosphere of the monastery, whereas for the stories of the past the narrator takes the listener(s) to some town, city or kingdom. The story of the past, therefore, constitutes a secular time and space. Now taking the narrative time to the past and the locale to a secular space is a technique to attain the consent of the listener:

> Thus they can be, and were probably meant to be read at a variety of levels, and function along lines of both common sense and Buddhist ethics, often welding the two together in complex, not always harmonious compositions.
>
> — Roy, 1996: 27

Thus, a distinction between the discursive and the narrative texts becomes apparent in the Jātaka fables. The discursive text takes its origin from the narrative of the present itself, in the religious gathering of the Buddha. The reason why the narrative is born is important to remember. There is some situation, conflict or problem, because of which the Buddha must respond with a solution. Instead of speaking plainly about the solution, the Buddha goes on and narrates a story from the past. It is the discursive content present in the statement of a problem at the beginning of each Jātaka that leads to the formation of the narrative text from the past. Once the narrative text is completed the discursive content again resurfaces in the form of the *gāthā*. So, the Jātaka fable moves from the discursive text to a narrative text and back to a discursive text. So, the present time is denoted by the discursive text and the past, which is always retold by the Buddha, by the narrative text.

Every story begins with a statement of what it is going to exemplify, and ends by drawing out the moral lesson (love even for foes; generous charity even in the time of great poverty, to the extent of even sacrificing one's own body and family; supreme courage in charity and in renunciation; empathy with suffering beings; purity of heart; right conduct; moral fortitude; steadfastness in *dharma*; purity of character; truth in all situations at any cost; detachment from greed and anger; acquisition of merit; love of virtue; forgiveness; forbearance; etc.). In fact, every narrative begins with a catch phrase or statement, which might be called the kernel of the narrative discourse. For instance, the *Maccha Jātaka* (No. 75) starts with the phrase, "Pajjunna, thunder!" which sets the tone for the narrative, as in the fable the *bodhisattva* born as the Fish prays successfully for rain.

In the *Pañcatantra* again, each fable can be broken into a narrative text, and discursive text. As the fables quote freely from the Śāstras, at times, the discursive text is so long that it grows almost independent of the narrative text. And, hence, the narrative and discursive units could be described as different texts within a single text. For example, the speech of Damanaka to Karataka in the first book is so detailed a discursive unit that it grows independent of the immediate situations in the narrative:

> Only they deserve to live whose life is inspiration and means of survival for several others. Otherwise, even birds get enough to eat and fill their belly by mere use of beak . . . those moving in all circles of people and serving to reduce their misery, like clouds bringing relief from hot Sun, are few in number . . . it has been said the king always listens to one nearest to him even if he be uneducated and illiterate . . . there are three types of persons — those who speak sweet words, hiding malice in their hearts; those who stay mute and non-committal; and those who use harsh words on any occasion requiring a precipitate response.
>
> — *The Pañcatantra*, 2006

The *Pañcatantra* is replete with such discursive harangues that stand out as separate units in the narrative. Here, Damanaka is actually addressing the listeners/readers as much as Karataka. The text implicates Karataka as a listener on behalf of the listener/reader of the text.

That the discourse influences the overall structure of the narrative becomes very apparent when the reader understands the connection between the frame-narrative and the inner narrative. The inner narrative, narrated by the characters of the frame-narrative, usually acts as an example to the other characters of the frame-narrative. The story often has symbolic and psychological pertinence for the characters in the outer story. There is definitely a parallel between the two stories, and it seems as if the fiction of the inner story is used to reveal the truth in the outer story. The inner narrative may bring to light the background of characters or events, tell of myths and legends and quote from the Śāstric texts to make a point about the character or situation in the outer narrative. On the contrary, the outer narrative may also prove critical in the interpretation of the inner narrative.

In "Karṇa-Parva," of the *Mahābhārata*, for instance, Śalya, Karṇa's charioteer, gives the great warrior some extremely useful discourses, during which he uses fables. Now, the fable-narrative narrated by him sheds greater light on Karṇa's problems. Here, primarily, the problem with him is nothing but his swollen pride and false confidence that he has gained due to the blind flattery of Dhṛtarāṣṭra's sons. Karṇa is underestimating Arjuna, and thinks his victory is certain. Śalya wants him to be realistic, or else he would face defeat and death at the hands of Arjuna and Kṛṣṇa. This issue in the frame-narrative is explained better by the fable-narrative that it contains, in the same way as the inner narrative can be better interpreted in the context of the narrative and the discursive background provided by the frame-narrative. Śalya narrates the fable of the Crow and the Swan to cure the great warrior of his "intoxicated self." He establishes the connection between the frame-narrative and the inner narrative at the very opening of the latter narrative, in the following words:

> Listen, O Karṇa, to this simile of a crow that I am about to narrate. Having heard it, thou mayest do what thou choosest, O thou that art destitute of intelligence and that art a wretch of thy race. I do not, O Karṇa, remember the slightest fault in me for which, O thou of mighty arms, thou mayest desire to slay my innocent self. I must tell thee what is for thy good and what is for thy ill, acquainted as I am with both, especially as I am the driver of thy car and desirous of the good of king Duryodhana.
>
> — *The Mahābhārata*, "Karṇa-Parva," Section 41

In the fable narrated by him, the Crow is swollen with pride and harbours a wrong impression of his strength, blinded as he is due to the flattery of the children who feed him daily. The children flatter him that he is the best among the birds, and no bird could fly as swift and as long a distance like him.

Like Karṇa, in the frame-narrative, he challenges the swans. The swans are born as the best flyers, equipped with the abililty to fly long distances. The Swan, like an ideal warrior who warns the weak opponent before the fight, advises him:

> The swans then, that were capable of going everywhere at will, addressed the crow, saying, "We are swans, having our abode in the Manasā Lake. We traverse the whole Earth, and amongst winged creatures we are always applauded for the length of the distances we traverse. Being, as thou art, only a crow, how canst thou, O fool, challenge a swan endued with might, capable of going everywhere at will, and doing large distances in course of his flight? Tell us, O crow, how thou shalt fly with us.

Intoxicated with blind confidence, the Crow gives an imaginary description of his unrealistic abilities:

> The crow said, I shall without doubt fly displaying a hundred and one different kinds of motion. Doing every hundred *yojana*s in a separate and beautiful kind of motion, I shall display all those motions. Rising up, and swooping down, and whirling around, and coursing straight, and proceeding gently, and advancing steadily, and performing the diverse courses up and receding back, and soaring high, and darting forward and soaring upwards with fiercer velocity, and once more proceeding gently and then proceeding with great impetuosity, and once again swooping down and whirling around and advancing steadily, and rising up by the jerks, and soaring straight, and once more falling down and wheeling in a circle and rushing proudly, and diverse other kinds of motion, these all I shall display in the sight of all of you. Ye shall then witness my strength.

As a part of the competition, both had to fly over the sea. Eventually, the Crow's body gives up, and he comes to realise, with his fatigue, his mistake. He looks for a treetop or some land to perch, but there is none to be seen. He gets scared for life and screams frantically for help from the Swan, who saves his life. The end of this fable again draws its connection with the frame-narrative, in the sense that both can be better interpreted by recourse to the other:

> Thus was that crow, fed on the remains of others' dinners, vanquished by the swan. The crow, then, casting off the pride of might and energy, adopted a life of peace and quiet. Indeed, even, as that crow, fed upon the remains of the dinners of the Vaiśya children, disregarded his equals and superiors, so dost thou, O Karṇa, that art fed by the sons of Dhṛtarāṣṭra upon the remains of their dishes, disregard all thy equals and superiors. Why didst thou not slay Pārtha at Virāṭa's city when thou hadst the advantage of being protected by Droṇa and Droṇa's son and Kṛpa and Bhīṣma and the other Kauravas? There where, like a pack of jackals defeated by a lion, ye all were defeated with great slaughter by the diadem-decked Arjuna, what became of your prowess? Beholding also thy brother slain by Savyasācī, in the very sight of the Kuru heroes, it was thou that didst fly away first. . . . As the crow (in the story), acting with intelligence, had sought the protection of the swan, so do thou seek the protection of him of Vṛṣṇi's race, and of Pāṇḍu's son Dhanañjaya. When thou shalt in battle behold Vāsudeva and Dhanañjaya, those two endued with great prowess, stationed together on the same car, thou shalt not then, O Karṇa, utter such speeches. . . .
>
> — *The Mahābhārata,* "Karṇa-Parva," Section 41

Along with the method of intercalating stories within stories, there is another method of story-telling, whose origin goes back to ancient India; it is that of mixing prose with verse in a narrative framework. This method has also been adopted by many writers throughout the world, even by some contemporary writers like Ama Aita Aidoo of Ghana. The art of mixing the prose first with the instructive epigrams and then with verses has been done for the first time in the Indian literature. There are critics who even argue that the epigrams and verses preceded the prose narrative. In other words, the fables earlier existed in the compressed verse form, and later got developed into prose narratives.

Therefore, as per this view, the origin of the fable is linked to the epigram and the poetic statement of instruction. Later, various gnomic stanzas were placed at the top of the fables, and since then gnomic stanzas have always been an important part of fable literature. The opinion of K. Mullenhoff on German fables is very relevant to the Indian fables:

> Many old German proverbs contain small animal-fables: the heron scolds water, because he cannot swim; if the mouse is fully fed, food tastes bitter, etc. More than one gnomic stanza were enlarged poetically into fables, so conversely many fables were abridged into gnomic stanzas.
>
> — in Winternitz, 1977: 34

H.J. Blackham in his book, *The Fable as Literature*, contends that there is a greater proximity between the structure of the fable-verses and a poem as an art form, and hence, the fable-verses contributed to the development of the poetic sense in literature around the world. It is because the verses were an integral part of the fables originally that we can draw a parallel between the form of a fable and a poem:

> In this respect the fable may seem, and has seemed, closer to poetic composition than to the fabricated histories of the story-teller. As each poem is said to have its own poetics, so has each fable its own ground of justification.
>
> — Blackham, 1985: 225

The conceptual term for the verse interspersed in the prose narrative is called *campū*. It is coined by Daṇḍin in his *Kāvyādarśa*. He writes a theoretical analysis of the genre of *kāvya* in mixed verse and prose form (*gadya-padyamayī*). Etymologically, therefore, the *campū* is a narrative in mixed prose and verse. Nothing is stated, however, on the relative content of verse and prose in a narrative. But as it is the prose text (*kathā* and *ākhyāyikā*) that includes the verse in its texture for a specific purpose, so it is a generally understood convention that the verse should not be stretched in the narrative beyond its immediate use.

It has always been discussed that broadly speaking an Indian fable can be classified into narrative text and discursive text. Now, more often than not, the prose is used in the narrative section and the verse in the discursive section of the fable. The earliest known text in the tradition of *campū* literature is Trivikrama Bhaṭṭa's *Nala Campū*, otherwise also known as *Damayantī Kathā*. It was composed in the tenth century CE, and narrates the grand story of Nala and Damayantī. Bhaṭṭa makes a good use of verse at important points in the narrative. The verses found in many of the prose narratives of Indian literature are so significant that they have held an independent importance by themselves, which is why they have been included in many metrical anthologies.

The *Hitopadeśa* makes a greater use of the *campū* form than all other versions of the *Pañcatantra*. Therefore, this version is given the name of a compilation, *Subhāṣita-saṅgraha*. The text has come to its present form only by interweaving the contents of the narratives with the aphorisms and verses from Cāṇakya and other sources, apart from the verses which the original *Pañcatantra* already contained. As a part of the oral tradition, one reason why verses were included in the narrative was their mnemonic value. The verses made it easier to remember the stories, as each had contained in it the message of an entire narrative. Ludwik Sternbach in his *Cāṇakya's Aphorisms in the*

Hitopadeśa classifies the stanzas in the text, and groups then into various categories:

(a) the king and his officials; state policy,

(b) wealth and property,

(c) knowledge and ignorance,

(d) virtue and vice,

(e) women in general and wives,

(f) sons,

(g) friends, foes and various types of association,

(h) guests and hosts,

(i) servants; service, and

(j) miscellaneous.

— Sternbach, 1956: 123

Hence, it is possible to analyse the verses in terms of the overall discourse of the compositions they are included in.

The practical wisdom of the *Pañcatantra* apart from being rendered in the narratives proper is more effectively conveyed by the means of verse, which has already been discussed. Now, whether the narrative verses had been there in the original work or were later interpolations is a matter of debate. The numerous versions of the *Pañcatantra* disagree in terms of the verse content. In later version of the work they are placed more closely and make frequent appearances, as in the *Hitopadeśa.* The narrative stanzas serve as the introduction and conclusion of the narratives, making them livelier. They also refer to the discourse, and substantiate the subject matter of the narrative, as for example the following verse from the *Hitopadeśa*:

A covetous man should be met with money;

An unbending man with humility;
One should humour the desires of a fool;
But an intelligent man should be addressed with truth.
— *The Hitopadeśa*, 1924: 195

In the Jātaka, the *gāthās* (verses) play an even more important role. The whole composition is classified in terms of the *gāthās* that each narrative contains. The narratives containing one verse (*ekanipāta*) make up the first book, and it goes on like that till the fourteenth book, after which have the Jātakas with 20, 30, or more verses, till the last section number 22, called *mahānipāta*, which contains narratives that contain hundreds of verses. The verses inserted in the prose narratives foreground the relationship between the narrator and the immediate listeners apart from serving the discursive function, which it always does. Also, in the context of form the verses are important because the Buddha, by recourse to them, takes the narrative outside the fictional framework, and addresses his listeners directly, as in the following verse from *Tittira Jātaka* (No. 37):

For they who honour age, in Truth are versed;
Praise now and bliss hereafter, is their meed.
— *The Jātaka*, 1990: 94

4

Indian Fables
Contemporary Theory

> But first "Fable" is the tale of invention, it recites and describes itself; it presents itself from the start as a beginning, the inauguration of a discourse or of a textual mechanism. It does what it says, not being content with announcing . . .
>
> — Jacques Derrida, 1992: 322

As an evidence of cross-cultural encounters and assimilation, the Indian fables reached different countries and communities across the world, and integrated into their cultural repertoire. It is worthwhile, therefore, to attempt a cross-cultural analysis by placing the narratives in relation to the contemporary theories of narrative from the West. There is no better text to quote from to understand the centrality of the narrative in the modern Western knowledge systems than Roland Barthe's *Introduction to the Structural Analysis of Narrative*:

> The Narratives of the world are numberless. Narrative is first and foremost a prodigious variety of genres, themselves distributed amongst different substances — as though any material were fit to receive man's stories . . . narrative is present in myth, legend, fable, tale, novella, epic, history, tragedy, drama, comedy, mime, painting (think of Carpassio's *Saint Ursula*), stained-glass windows, cinema, comics, news items, conversation. Moreover, under this almost infinite diversity of forms, narrative is present in

> every age, in every place, in every society; it begins with the very history of mankind and there nowhere is nor have been a people without narrative. — Barthes, 1977: 79

India boasts of a rich narrative tradition, the fable tradition being one strand in this tradition, the universality of which, both in terms of time and space, is revealed in the way the narratives lend themselves to the theoretical models of analysis developed in the twentieth century in the West. What is even more interesting, however, is that the Indian texts, themselves, internalise theoretical systems of various types that compare with the conceptual categories of structuralism, post-structuralism, postmodernism, etc.

For the experts and the common readers alike, it is intriguing as to how the various texts of the Indian tradition, including the collection of fables, have survived so long so intact. The reason, which the texts make apparent, is that they are open to the mutability of the time. Being part of an oral tradition, the texts are not restricted within an elite domain closed by the signature of the author. A text once composed in the Indian tradition is collectively owned, discussed, disseminated, and commented upon. In this sense, they have been referred to in the previous chapters as de-authored texts, rather than copyright creations of the authors.

In the Indian tradition, the texts display "the relativisation of the relation of the writer, the reader, and the observer" (Barthes, 1977: 156). The *Mahābhārata* is a wonderful case in point. The text, in the oral form has come down to us through the cumulative efforts of Gaṇeśa, Vyāsa, the Sūtas, the Bhr̥gus, and the many later compilers who included the mini narratives in the epic. But, who is the author of the *Mahābhārata*?

It is not important for an Indian mind to associate a text with an author. Since the very beginning, the compositions have developed with the mutable relationship among the various composers, the listeners, and the commentators. Generation after generation a new relationship between the narrator and the listener or (the reader) keep the text circulating in the culture. The varying layers of the narrator-listener relationship that dilutes the author-centric approach is mentioned in the *Mahābhārata*:

> Śaunaka said, "O son, thou hast narrated to me this extensive and great history commencing from the progeny of Bhṛgu. O son of *Sūta*, I have been much gratified with thee. I ask thee again, to recite to me, O son of a *Sūta*, the history composed by Vyāsa. The varied and wonderful narrations that were recited amongst those illustrious *sadasya*s assembled at the sacrifice, in the intervals of their duties of that long-extending ceremony, and the objects also of those narrations, I desire to hear from thee, O son of a *Sūta*! Recite therefore, all those to me fully."
>
> Sauti said, "The brāhmaṇas, in the intervals of the duties, spoke of many things founded upon the Vedas. But Vyāsa recited the wonderful and great history called the *Bharata*."
>
> — *The Mahābhārata*, "Adi-Parva," Section LIX

Vyāsa is not the author, but only the reciter. And, as is evident from this quotation, even the mini narratives, the fables in the *Mahābhārata* recited by Bhīṣma or Vidura from the folk, are neither created by them nor by the narrator of the epic as a whole.

Likewise, if we consider Viṣṇu Śarmā as the author of the fables, in the sense of a creator, what about the narratorial voice that narrates Viṣṇu Śarmā himself and the fables attributed to him in the text? *Pañcatantra* fables are not an expression of the stories created by an author for a specific audience, the princes. In fact, both the narrator and the immediate listeners are only one of the many instances of the narration of the fables in specific situations. This is attested by the fact that quite a few fables from the text have come from Jātakas and many other sources, which questions in another way the authorial purity of the work. The issue of intertextuality related to this is discussed later. Hence, *Pañcatantra*, in all its versions and adaptations, is a typical instance of the Indian text that is primarily about the circulation of the text itself, regardless of the particular importance of the author or the reader.

In terms of the language brought from the postmodernist theory, the fables are primarily about creating an opening where the authorial subject continuously disappears. In *Pañcatantra*, there is an impression as if Viṣṇu Śarmā is the composer, but in *Hitopadeśa*, Nārāyaṇa becomes the compiler and Viṣṇu Śarmā is relegated to the status of a narrator. But even the narrator's responsibility is taken away from him as there are several narrators all the time entering through the fabric of the text. For instance, in the first book, from Viṣṇu Śarmā to the fox-brothers Damanaka and Karataka to the Sparrow, Tiṭibhi, the narratorial position is constantly shifting, thereby making the fixed position of not only the author but also the narrator problematic. Michel Foucault in the beginning of his essay, "What is an Author?" says:

> The coming into being of the notion of "author" constitutes the privileged moment of individualisation in the history of ideas, knowledge, literature, philosophy, and the sciences. Even today, when we reconstruct the history of a concept, literary genre, or school of philosophy, such categories seem relatively weak, secondary, and superimposed sanctions in comparison with the solid and fundamental unit of the author and the work. — Foucault, 1989: 263

In the Indian tradition, there is no such "privileged moment of individualisation" encountered. The fable-narratives in Jātakas might seem close to an assertion of an individual author, the Buddha, whose individuality might appear to have dominated the form and the reception of the stories in the Indian culture. But even in this case, there is no question of identifying the Buddha as the single most important narrator-author. As it has been discussed in chapter one, for more than 800 years, at least from the third century BCE to the fifth century CE, when Buddhaghoṣa gave Jātakas their final shape, there had been no need to bring the signature of the Buddha's individuality for the dissemination of the fables. In fact, ironically it was the excessive freedom of the stories outside the influence of the author-narrator that made it important for the later compilers and writers to give a tangible shape to them. Again, the concern was not that they should be compiled so as to conform exactly to what the Buddha had said. They were compiled during the last of the various Buddhist councils in order to prevent the distortion of the *dhamma*. But even after they were written down, the texts have been received more in the oral form.

The Buddha narrated the fables following the oral tradition, and, it is well understood that in India all the saints who teach morals in the form of stories considered themselves as vehicles of the already existing knowledge. There is no importance attached to the fact whether the narratives or the discourses originate from the self, even if it is the self of the Buddha or, say, Guru Nānak. The knowledge as a structure is beyond them, and they become only the medium to bring the knowledge to the masses. It is a part of the Indian popular lore that once a *yogī* asked Guru Nānak "who is your *guru*?" to which Nānak replied, "the Word is the Guru and the mind attuned to the Word is the disciple." Likewise, *Taittirīya Brāhmaṇa* states,

> All the gods, the celestial spirits, men and animals live in the Word. In the Word all the worlds find their support.
>
> — quoted in Panikkar, 2001: II.8.84

As a Jātaka fable starts, the narrator-Buddha makes it clear that he is only making known the already existing historical narrative from the past, about which the disciples and the other listeners are unaware but which does already exist apart from and prior to him. In the *Lakkhana Jātaka* (No. 11), the Buddha begins the narrative in the characteristic Jātaka convention:

> Once upon a time in the city of Rājagṛha in the kingdom of Magadha there ruled a certain king, in whose days the *bodhisattva* came to life as a stag. Growing up, he dwelt in the forest as the leader of the herd of a thousand deer. He had two young ones named Luckie and Blackie. When he grew old, he handed his charge over to his two sons, placing 500 deer under the care of each of them. And so now these two young stags were in charge of the herd.
>
> — *The Jātaka*, 1990: 35

As is apparent, the narrator here not only provides absolute objectivity by roping in the reference to the king and the milieu, but also makes it very clear that what he is narrating is not his conception, but only a narration of an experience from his earlier life, which is unknown to those who lack such divine vision. It is the history which is presented as the narrative. When he ends the narrative, he again makes it clear that he is not inserting anything to appropriate an already existing historical narrative:

> Such was the *bodhisattva*'s welcome to his son; and after living to a good old age, he passed away to fare according to his deserts. — *The Jātaka*, 1990: 36

But the question is, if the narrative as a story or as a discourse exists independent of the author in the Indian tradition, then why is the reference to author-narrator as a vehicle of narrative-dissemination important? Samuel Beckett, the renowned Irish dramatist, has the answer when he says, "'What does it matter who is speaking,' someone said that 'what does it matter who is speaking'" (quoted in Foucault, 1989: 264). The same indifference to the question of the author is to be found in the Indian texts.

The author-function, to use Foucault's term, is invoked in the Indian tradition only as a signifier, a name, to tag the narratives with. It is made very clear in the beginning of *Pañcatantra* that Viṣṇu Śarmā is not the author, in the sense of a creator. He is the one who has mastered the discourses of the Upaniṣads, the Purāṇas and the Dharmaśāstras. He is the one who, however, knows the codes that govern these discourses, and can represent them in a narrative form. He is an expert knower rather than an author. To go back to Foucault, "even when an individual has been accepted as an author, we must ask whether everything he wrote, said, or left behind is part of his work" (Foucault, 1989: 265).

In *Pañcatantra*, Viṣṇu Śarmā is given the name of an author only to achieve the materiality for the text. There is an explicit statement that everything that he narrated, in fact, came from the discourses which were already told by many other thinkers and story-tellers before him. In a characteristic Indian manner, Viṣṇu Śarmā, in the beginning of the text, disowns his claim, so to say his copyright, over the text, and attributes the contents to many who have uttered the discourses before him:

> The author also offers obeisance to proto-sages Manu, Bṛhaspati, Śukrācārya, Parāśara, and his son Vyāsa, sage Cāṇakya and others who laid the ground rules for continuance of society. — *The Pañcatantra*, 2006: 11

It is made known that the text is only a rearrangement, in

narrative form, of the discourses already existing, as uttered by the various thinkers of the Indian tradition.

Similarly, the Buddha functions more as a signifier for the narratives around which the stories could be arranged. He does attribute legitimacy to the narratives, but not as the one who created them, but as the one who simply narrated them:

> The story was told by the Master in the Bamboo grove near Rājagṛha about Devadatta. . . . Devadatta, through failing to carry the Five Points which he had pressed for, had made a schism in the Brotherhood and had gone off with 500 Brethren to dwell at Gayā-sisa . . . the Master, knowing this, called the two chief disciples and said. . . .
>
> — *The Jātaka*, 1990: 34

This theoretical position of describing the Buddha or Viṣṇu Śarmā just as another narrative device is not much distant from some of the recent researches in the West on the Greek literature. As our texts, the Greek texts are also difficult to pin down to a single author. In the introduction to a recent translation of *Odyssey*, Thomas R. Walsh and Rodney Merrill put forth a simple question, "What is meant by the name Homer (Bennet, 2005: 32)?" Some critics argue that Homer simply functions as a figure of speech in the text. To quote Andrew Bennet,

> This difficulty in thinking about the "first" poet in the European literary tradition is a consequence not just of a lack of records but of the very status of the poet in the oral culture in which he is or they are understood to have worked . . . every performance in the oral epic tradition constitutes a new composition, that every performance is unique, and that at the same time every performance is also embedded within the tradition. — Bennet: 2005: 32

This is exactly the case with the Indian texts, as ours has also been predominantly an oral tradition.

This whole debate around the author began to surface in the West with Barthes' landmark essay, *The Death of the Author* (1967), because of an anxiety to break free of constraints imposed by the self/other dichotomy. An act of reading in that tradition is a contest between the reader and text, and hence an allergy to the so-called authorial oppression in the act of reading a text. "The author in this model not only "owns" the text but owns guarantees, originates, its meanings, its interpretations" (Bennet, 2005: 15). Hence, Barthes and other postmodernists have made an effort to liberate the text from the authorial prison-house:

> . . . *The Death of the Author*, then, abolishes authorial voice, eliminates voice as origin and source, voice as identity, unity . . . by describing the modern author as "scriptor," and displacing the meaning from the author to the text, Barthes is able to argue that readers will be liberated from the oppressive control of authorial consciousness and critical guardianship.
>
> — Bennet, 2005: 12-15

A reference to *Pañcatantra* makes Barthes' notion of the "scriptor" pretty clear. Viṣṇu Śarmā is no more than a "scriptor," a go-between the different knowledge-texts (on culture, polity, art, and administration) and the masses. At best, he is the illustrator; a skilled knower who could illustrate the knowledge of these disciplines through narratives. The position being the originator is never his, but in any case, it has never been a privileged position in the Indian tradition.

This brings us to the related issue of the dynamics of textual interlinking in the Indian fables. The various fable-texts, as discussed in chapter one, were in wide circulation in and around the third century BCE, and hence there is a great deal of overlapping of the textual space evident in the case of some of the fables. This whole issue can be discussed in the context of the theory of intertextuality as found in the contemporary theory. Intertextuality, as a theory, talks about the cumulative formation of the various texts of a culture or cultures in general.

Julia Kristeva is the first theorist who coined the term "intertextuality" in her essays, "The Bounded Text," and "Word, Dialogue, and Novel", both of which were first published in 1969. By "intertextuality," she means

> . . . to indicate that a text (such as a novel, a poem or historical document) is not a self-contained or autonomous entity, but is produced from other texts. The interpretation that a particular reader generates from a text will then depend on the recognition of the relationship of the given text to other texts. — Edgar and Sedgwick, eds., 1999: 197

She discusses literary texts in terms of two axes: a *horizontal axis*, which connects the author and reader of a text, and a *vertical axis*, which links the text to other texts. Now, there are several codes that unite these two axes, which are shared by all the other texts. For reading any text, therefore, an understanding of the codes of other texts is equally important. Kristeva asserts that "every text is from the outset under the jurisdiction of other discourses which impose a universe on it" (Chandler, "Intertextuality," http://www.aber.ac.uk/media/Documents/S4B/sem09.html. Accessed on 15-2-2005).

This theoretical postulation is quite in consonance with the Indian fables, and other narratives of the Indian tradition. In fact, intertextuality applies more to an oral tradition than to a written tradition, because in the oral tradition the texts are always already on a move in every single act of reading or performance. As discussed in chapter 2, the narratives of the Indian fable have never been frozen by the written word. The Indian folklore has developed the popular stories in various Indian vernaculars by adopting the stories from the fable composition like the *Pañcatantra*, the *Hitopadeśa*, the Jātakas, and the like. And these adaptations or adoptions have never been an academic activity, performed by deliberate minds. But indeed, there has been a natural process of assimilation between different cultural texts of India. How can we perhaps account for the presence of narrative motifs from a *Pañcatantra* fable in the folk tale of a certain region unless there has been a natural process of negotiation among the various Indian narratives? Thus, the Indian fable and non-fable narratives are highly intertextual, which "may be understood as the thesis that no text exists outside its continuing interpretation and reinterpretation" (Chandler, "Intertextuality," http://www.aber.ac.uk/media/Documents/S4B/sem09.html. Accessed on 15-2-2005).

The intertextuality of Indian fables would not be possible unless their oral form of transmission made them operate simultaneously as an interactive field. It is very interesting to note how a single narrative found in the Jātakas could do rounds both in the *Mahābhārata* and the *Pañcatantra* as well as in the modern Indian folklore, with varying meanings and implications. It goes on only to show that narratives co-exist in the oral tradition that facilitates a higher degree of textual exchanges. Having said that, this argument comes very close to Roland Barthes' formulation of a "text," which he compares with a "Work," in his essay, "From Work to Text":

> The text is not to be thought of as an object that can be computed . . . the work is a fragment of substance, occupying a part of the space of books (in a library, for example), the text is a methodological field . . . the text is a process of demonstration, speaks according to certain rules (or against certain rules); the work can be held in hand, the text is held in language, only exists in the movement of a discourse (or rather, it is Text for the very reason that it knows itself as text). . . .
>
> — Barthes, 1997: 156-57

Exactly this is how we understand that the Indian fables expand their methodological field by encapsulating various spheres of textual exchanges and performance. La Fontaine does not at all exaggerate when he says, in a preface to the second collection of his fables, that a greater part of his work he owes to the *Pañcatantra*. This is not simply a case of conscious borrowing — that is how a written tradition works — but a case of textual codes entering different spheres of culture.

As discussed in the previous chapters, the research findings of Theodor Benfey confirm the common textual sphere of the Indian fables. There are many instances of the narratives of the Jātakas and the *Pañcatantra*, especially, criss-crossing one another's textual contours. It is on the evidence of intertextual connections that Benfey claims the *Pañcatantra* to be a Buddhist work. One another indicator of the fable's freedom from the composer and its free life in the site of textuality is that with time, as various versions of the *Pañcatantra* came up, the intertextual connection became more prominent. The fact that the insertion from the Jātakas is to be found in the Syriac version of the *Pañcatantra* goes on to show that the journey of a text over time is fraught with relations with the other texts of the culture.

Clear intertexual connections can be seen among the Jātaka fable No. 361, the frame-narrative of the Lion and the Bull in the first book of the *Pañcatantra* and a modern folk narrative included in Walter Skeat's *Fables and Folk Tales From an Eastern Forest*, as discussed in a different context in chapter 2. However, the use of narrative in all these texts is not simply a case of simple borrowing. Though critics believe the Jātaka fable is the original source of this fable, the stories in the other two texts are not naïve adaptations. The modern folk tale, as collected by Skeat, is different from the Buddhist Jātaka in the sense that the Jackal is not accepted in the friendship of the Lion and the Bull. Likewise, in this modern tale, it is the Lion who kills the Bull by his roar, whereas in the *Pañcatantra*, the Bull's roar made the Lion scared to self-decimation. The fable found in the *Pañcatantra* differs from the modern folk fable in the sense that the Lion and the Bull are not friends before the appearance of the Jackal on the scene, and only the Bull is killed in the fight. Again, a variant in which the estrangement is not successful is to be found in the Jātaka No. 361.

So, intertextuality is not about one text being borrowed from another text. It is equally not about the one text being influenced by another text:

> [t]he concept . . . has been generally misunderstood. It has nothing to do with matters of influence by one writer upon another, or with the sources of a literary work. . . . It is defined in [Kristeva's] *La Revolution du langage poetique* [1974] as the transposition of one or more systems of signs into another. . . . "Any signifying practice is a field (in the sense of space traversed by lines of force) in which various signifying systems undergo such a transposition." — Roudiez, 1984: 15

Hence, intertextuality has nothing to do with matters of influence of one writer upon another, or with sources of literary work; it actually involves the assimilation of components of a textual system, for instance the motifs found in the fables. The whole process is defined in *La Revolution du Langage Poetique* as the transposition of the system of signs into different textual systems, which give birth to new articulations all the time, a new development of systems. In "The Bounded Text," Kristeva, again, argues that in the textual space of a given text many utterances from other texts meet and neutralise one another.

Therefore, the interdiscursive references found in the texts assume on the part of the readers prior knowledge about them. In the Indian fables, we are concerned more about the fable motifs which are constantly shared across different texts, because of the oral narrative practice. The motifs function more as signs, with shifting meanings, and therefore, we are not talking about the entire story being represented in different texts, but the motifs and cultural meanings being transposed from one text to another. As for example, the Lion-Bull episode and its variant spread in different texts. The motif of the wild roar, for instance, enters as an important meaning-unit in *Sigāla Jātaka* (No. 152). In the *Pañcatantra*, the Lion is horrified almost to death because of the Bull's roar; in the modern folk tale, it is the roar of the Lion that kills the Bull; in the Jātaka, the roar of the Lion kills the Jackal. Now, all these texts exist in a simultaneous textual framework through the transposition of the roar-sign from one text to another. In the Jātaka, it is the *bodhisattva* who is born as the Lion, and uses the roar as a strategy to kill the Jackal, which his brothers failed to do:

> . . . the Lion continued: "My brothers wanted to kill this Jackal, but knew not how to lay their plans cleverly; so they leapt up too quickly at him, and so came by their death. This I will not do; but I will make the Jackal burst his own heart as he lies there in the Crystal Cave." So he espied out the path whereby the Jackal used to go up and down, and turning that way he roared thrice the lion's roar, that earth and heaven together were all one great roaring! The Jackal lying in the Crystal Cave was frightened and astounded, so that his heart burst and he perished on the spot incontinently. — *The Jātaka*, 1990, Book II: 6

This motif again transposes into the text of the *Sabbadatha Jātaka* (No. 241), where we come across the following passage, which describes the *bodhisattva*:

> So he tapped with his foot on the Lion which he sat upon to roar. And the Lion resting his mouth upon the Elephant's temple, roared thrice, without any matter of doubt. The elephants were terrified and dropped the Jackal down at their feet; they trampled upon his head and crushed it to atoms. — *The Jātaka*, 1990, Book II: 170

So, it is in fact the meaning-units that enter the different texts, and this particular motif, found in the Jātaka, the *Pañcatantra*, and modern folk tale, could be seen as an example of intertextuality in the Indian fables.

W. Norman Brown in his *The Pañcatantra in the Modern Indian Folklore* gives an estimate of 3000 small narratives from India (contemporary India), Sri Lanka, Burma, Tibet and Malaysia that have developed over the centuries from early Indian tales found in the *Pañcatantra*. This is a good indicator of the intertextuality that governs the development of the Indian narratives. Some of the fables change their characters as they enter different cultures, but the motif as the meaning system is transposed without much change. As for example, the motif of rash killing of a loyal animal, where the Indian Mongoose becomes the Dog once the fable enters the narrative space of the European cultures, but the primary meaning that is to be communicated remains the same, though the ancillary meaning takes on different implications depending upon the new narrative contexts of each narrative in the target culture.

Another indicator of intertextuality of the Indian fables is the presence of references and quotations from the various knowledge-texts that re-form themselves in the new narrative contexts of the fable-narratives. For example, Cāṇakaya verses complied by Ludwik Sternbach in his *Cāṇakya-Nīti-Text Tradition* that have been discussed in chapter 2. Now, most of the Cāṇakya verses and those in the *Mahābhārata* have been absorbed in the Indian society in the form of proverbs, and their entry into the text of the Indian fable endorses Kristeva's view that "any text is constructed as a mosaic of quotations; any text is the absorption and transformation of another" (quoted in Brydon, 1999, "Intertextuality in Timothy Findley's Headhunter," *Journal of Canadian Studies*, Winter 1998 1999, http://findarticles.com/p/articles/mi_qa3683 is_199801/ai_n8774689/p3. Accessed on 12-11-2006). Thus, the Indian fable-narrative is often "plural," to use Barthes' term. We might take the following verses from *Cāṇakya Compendia of Verses* and the *Mahābhārata* (already cited in Chapter 2), and discuss the intertextual connections:

(a) Be not too straight, but look to the woods.
Straight trees are cut but the crooked stand.
— Sternbach, 1963-64; Cāṇakya Verse 6.5

(b) You should give up a man for a family,
Give up a family for a village,
Give up a village for a country,
But sell out the world for yourself.
— Sternbach, 1963-64; Cāṇakya Verse 1.7

Now, the assimilation of these two verses in the *Hitopadeśa* makes the fable-text "plural." In the post-structuralist/postmodernist sense the plurality of the text does not simply mean the presence of more than one meaning, as finding the Cāṇakya sayings or Kāmandaka's verses in *Pañcatantra* would imply at an obvious level:

> The text is not a coexistence of meanings but a passage, an overcrossing; thus it answers not to an interpretation, even a liberal one, but to an explosion, a dissemination. The plural of the text depends, that is, not on the ambiguity of its contents but on what might be called the stereographic plurality of its weave of signifiers (etymologically, the text is a tissue, a woven fabric). — Barthes, 1977: 159

The fable is dense with meanings that require readings at various levels. Though at various levels the quotations from the knowledge-texts that are used by the fabulists are acknowledged, at times there is no clear statement on the origin of the source idea or motif.

Hence, the reader might acquire a prominent position in delving out the intertextual connections which are embedded. The idea of the frame-narrative of the third book of the *Pañcatantra* has come from the *Mahābhārata*. The *Pañcatantra* apparently does not mention it, but in the post-structuralist interpretation of the fable, we might delve out the signifying system of the *Pañcatantra,* which has modified the ethical standpoint of the *Mahābhārata* fable while co-opting its narrative resources. As already discussed in chapter 2, the fable in the *Mahābhārata* and the *Pañcatantra* belong to two entirely different world views. The fight between the owls and the crows as witnessed by Aśvatthāmā does face ethical questioning, but not so is the case in the *Pañcatantra.* What is important in terms of theory discussed is that like this particular instance, there are various places in the Indian fables where references from the other texts are not openly acknowledged but depend upon the reading activity to delve out not the source of the fable but the intertextual performances of the text that the reader is interpreting:

> The intertextual in which every text is held, it itself being the text-between of another text, it is not to be confused with some origin of the text: to try to find the "sources," the "influences" of a work is to fall in with the myth of filiations; the citations which go to make up a text are anonymous, untraceable, and yet *already read*: they are quotations without inverted commas. — Barthes, 1977: 160

There are different citations from Śāstras on different aspects of polity and practical living in the *Pañcatantra,* and the

Hitopadeśa, which are anonymous, and yet they make the authority of the Śāstras visible in the narrative.

This leads us to another aspect of the postmodernist poetics as reflected in the Indian fables — the decentring of narrative. A fable never attempts a totalisation of the narrative elements by subjecting them to a single paradigm. In other words, at different occasions a narrative flow is broken, decentred, and diversified to accommodate various discourses. This is a very important element in postmodernism as argued by Linda Hutcheon in her *A Poetics of Postmodernism*. Its typical case can be seen in *Pañcatantra*, where the fables, in the middle of their course, would pause and pick up a passage from Cāṇakya or Bharata Muni or Nārada, and then return again to the narrative line, and complete the narrative process.

Such decentring is because of the pressure of the discourse on the narrative, which makes it important for it to bring the portions from the discursive texts into the narrative framework. Most of the time the narrative is diversified with the inclusion of the poetic passages that bring a discourse, which though related to the narrative often grow independent of it. For instance, in the third fable of the third book of *Pañcatantra*, we come across a story about the Rabbit and the Elephant. Now in the middle of the narrative, the structure breaks to accommodate a discourse given by Manu:

> For his own protection the king should, without a second thought, abandon the land that provides him comfort and is full of harvestable land and capable of rearing animals . . . in times of peril, one must amass wealth. . . .
>
> — *The Pañcatantra*, 2006: 215-16

Instances like this make the Indian fable an eclectic assimilation of diverse narrative threads. The use of verse is marked in these narratives. In fact *gāthā*s (verse) appear frequently in these narratives, often breaking the narrative flow, but contributing important thoughts to the story.

The discursive use of *gāthā*s (the verses), as discussed in chapter 3 in detail, is another aspect of the Indian fables that takes them closer to another postmodernist theory associated with the name of Mikhail Bakhtin. His views expressed in the essay, "Discourse in the Novel," is more relevant to this context. In this essay, Bakhtin discusses on the questions of literary genres in terms of his famous concept of dialogic form. In a broader sense, he discusses the relationship between language and discourse, and argues that language as a form of social communication always include more than the speaking subject the voices of the immediate listener and other individual and social voices. And hence, language is always, at least the language as operative in the society, dialogic. To enumerate on this, he makes a distinction between prose and poetic forms used in literature, and contends that the language of novel (prose) is dialogic, whereas the poetic language is monologic.

In other words, he contends that prose is "centrifugal," as it is related to history and connects to the other social voices, whereas poetry is "centripetal"; it is primarily about a self-contained language that draws only on itself to attain an autonomous aesthetics:

> The poet is a poet insofar as he accepts the idea of a unitary and singular language and a unitary, monologically sealed-off utterance. These ideas are immanent in the poetic genres with which he works. . . . The poet must assume a complete single-person hegemony over his own language . . . there must be no distance between the poet and his word.
>
> — Bakhtin, 2002: 234

Poetry found in the Indian fables functions quite contrary to

Bakhtin's formulations. Poetry in the Indian fables is primarily a folk poetry, or poetry as an integral part of a prose narrative, that too of the fable, so it operates as a social discourse. Bakhtin's views are about poetry more complete as an art form, rather than poetic utterances. But, whatever be the case, poetry in the Jātakas and the *Pañcatantra* assume a very prominent discursive form. In fact, it is more social, and more dialogic than the prose.

In fact, it is poetry which brings the narrative back to the social sphere of the readers from the imaginative world of the animal characters. In the Jātakas, the complete discourse is described in explicit terms in verse, as for instance in the following passage from the *Kharadiya Jātaka* (No. 15), where the *bodhisattva* born as the head of a herd of deer says he can teach only the able listeners:

> For when a deer has twice four hoofs to run
> And branching antlers armed with countless tines,
> And when by seven tricks he's saved himself,
> I teach him then, Kharadiya, no more.
>
> — *The Jātaka*, 1990: 47

It is in such poetic passages that the central message of the narrative is expressed, and moreover, often, these passages become an integral part of the folk so that the narrative itself is identified by the poetry contained in it. Hence, the distinction between prose and poetry as formulated by Bakhtin does not hold ground in the context of the Indian fables.

However, his general views on literary prose is very helpful in the discussion of an important element of the Indian fable. "Discourse Typology in Prose" is an essay about the linguistic devices used in the literary prose, especially about the use of parody and dialogue. Bakhtin makes a significant statement in the second paragraph of the essay:

> Despite the fundamental differences among them, all these devices have one feature in common: in all of them discourse maintains a double focus, aimed at the referential object of speech, as in ordinary discourse, and simultaneously at a second context of discourse, a second speech act by another addresser. — Bakhtin, 1987: 285

Bakhtin makes a fundamental distinction between ordinary prose which makes a direct reference to one object, as its language operates within what he calls, "the bounds of a single monologic context," and a literary discourse in which there are multiple levels at which language works, in which, for instance, a dialogue does not refer to someone or something directly, but leads to another dialogue, another language. The language of the Indian fable, primarily because it uses so diversified material, is double-edged. A character, in some of the narratives, speaks to another character not about something but about another language. In other words, the texture of the Indian fables is replete with multiplicity of utterances. The narratives provide instances "of doubly oriented discourse" (Bakhtin, 1987: 286).

The fourth story in the third book of the *Pañcatantra* has already been discussed in another context. It serves well also to examine the polyphonic nature of this fable. In Bakhtin's terms, the narrative, as many other fables found in the *Pañcatantra,* constantly refers to myriad discourses. To begin with, we have the congenial friendship of Kapiñjala the Sparrow and the Crow. However, their friendly dialogues more than referring to things of ordinary life and making direct references, lead to other discourses of *maharṣis, ṛṣis,* and scriptures. This is again left undeveloped, the Sparrow disappears, and his abode in the hollow of the tree is occupied by the Rabbit. When the Sparrow returns dispute takes place and legal discourse is brought in. With their going to the Cat for legal advice, again discourse on *dharma* is roped in.

The point that is intended here is that all these varied discourses in the narrative are to a great extent independent of one another, one discourse becomes a cog for another discourse. There are multiple "speech acts" in the narrative and few are extremely contradictory. It really is a challenge how to analyse the multiple discursive strands in the same narrative communicated by various linguistic devices like dialogue and parody:

> Inevitably there will arise the question as to whether, and how, heterogeneous types of word-usage may be combined within a single context. On these grounds, a whole set of new stylistic problems arises; problems which until now stylistics has failed to take into account. As concerns style in prose, it is precisely these problems that have a paramount significance — Bakhtin, 1987: 286

A case of extreme heterogeneity of language used in the fable is the parody of the Buddhist concept of *ahiṁsā* and other religious precepts by the Cat, uttered in the religious language of the scriptures, which essentially contradict her dialogue with the Sparrow and the Crow where she talks about eating them. Whatever is the case, the point that Bakhtin puts across and which is reflected in the Indian fables is the presence of multiple discursive levels within the single narrative space, often including contending voices.

Quite close to this issue is the analysis of the way the narratives structure themselves in order to communicate a set of meanings. A discussion of the Indian fables in the context of the Western narratology might be an interesting experience to explore the narrative aspect of the fables. Narratology has developed as a distinct school in the contemporary theory with a lot of influence on the way literature and other cultural forms are studied and interpreted in the context of their narrativity. Theorists associated with this field are all big names in contemporary Western theory — Claude Lévi-Strauss, Vladimir Propp, Boris Tomashevsky, Tzvetan Todorov, Roland Barthes, Gerard Gennette, Seymour Chatman, and others.

In chapter 2, it has been discussed that the Indian fables require double readings to reveal the inherent meanings under the façade of the fable form. The fable, as is obvious about its form, operates on the literal level of meaning, and then on the metaphorical level as well. It is on the close second reading that the reader gets to comprehend the discourse immanent in the fable. This second reading amounts to reading the narrative as a whole, connecting the basic narrative to the discursive statements in the form of verses, and also checking the connections between the story and the frame-narrative.

The sixth fable in the last book of the *Pañcatantra*, for instance, is about the friendship of the fishes Śatabuddhi and Sahasrabuddhi, and the Frog Ekabuddhi. On the literal level, the narrative is about the unfortunate capture of the fishes by the fishermen due to their not heeding to the earlier advice of the Frog-friend to shift to some other pond as the fishermen were coming with their nets. On the second level the narrative exposes the contradiction between wisdom and blind knowledge, as expressed by the references to the passages from Cāṇakya in the story, and by placing this story within the frame-narrative that communicates the consequences of hasty action. The real intent of the text is communicated by the contradiction expressed by the following Cāṇakya verse,

> There is no place in this world that is beyond the reach of the virtues of a wise man, as Cāṇakya destroyed the sword waving Nanda dynasty using his intellect.

> Even those places can be immediately accessed by the wisdom of a wise man which are inaccessible even to air and light. — *The Pañcatantra*, 2006: 337

Again, what the Frog says to his wife seeing the fisherman carrying the two supposedly wise fishes with him is significant:

> O dear! Look Śatabuddhi is being carried on the head and Sahasrabuddhi is hanging from the shoulder while I Ekabuddhi, one with a single virtue, is sporting here in clean water. — *The Pañcatantra*, 2006: 338

It is the connection between the narrative units that brings out the narrative intent. The contemporary narrative theories are based on the various distinctions of the nature of what appears and what is embedded in the narrative structure. Most of the theories of the narrative are based on the two basic linguistic distinctions, *langue* and *parole* as developed by Saussure and *competence* and *performance* as developed by Chomsky, by which it is to be implied that the story is an abstract thing before it is articulated in the systemic world of the narrated text. Though there are critics like Todorov who argue that there is no meaning, no structure possible to be identified before being articulated. However, more generally the theorists believe that any given narrative has a *surface structure* and a *deep structure*, to use Chomsky's terms, and each has in his/her own way discussed this distinction.

For instance, Lévi-Strauss in his *The Structural Study of Myth* analyses a myth-narrative as made up of units put together according to certain rules. He states that these units make up relation with each other on the basis of binary pairs or opposites, which give the basis of the structure of the narrative. This again shows a distinction between an apparent structure of the narrative and the structure hidden, the unravelling of which leads to new meanings. Drawing on Strauss' method we can discuss the Indian fables, especially those in the *Yogavāsiṣṭha*. At a deeper level the fable featuring the Crow can be interpreted using the concept of binary opposition. In the text the binaries of characters such as Crow/Cuckoo, Crow/Crab, Rook/Owl, Crows/Cranes, and Cocks/Vultures could be interpreted, as between the first two in the following excerpt:

> It is better for you O clamorous crow to rend ears of those with your cracking voice that are not tired with splitting the head of others with their wily verbiage.
>
> The cuckoo associating with the crow, and resembling him in figure and colour, is distinguished by his sweet notes from the other; as learned man makes himself known by his speech in the society of the ignorant.
>
> — *The Yogavāsiṣṭha of Vālmīki*, 1998: 419

The philosophical discourse of the text can be discussed by foregrounding the systemic arrangement of the narrative units on the basis of binary oppositions.

The systemic arrangement of narrative units is common to most of the contemporary narrative theories. Hence, the distinction between the raw structure available during a general reading and the systemic structure revealed during a structural analysis of the narrative is communicated by the use of synonymous terms by various theorists: *fabula* and *sjuzhet* by the Russian formalists Propp and Tomashevsky, *histoire* and *discours* by the French Benveniste and Barthes, and *story* and *discourse* by the English narratologist Chatman. In all these, the first term is a simple description of the fundamental events of the story in their actual chronological order, while the second term denotes the conscious rearrangement of the fundamental events of the story and involves complex shifting of the narrative units in terms of time, space and characters.

All these theorists understand that each and every narrative has two levels of narrative arrangements. For instance, A.J. Greimas stresses on

> recognising and accepting the necessity of a fundamental distinction between two levels of representation and analysis: an *apparent* level of narration, at which the manifestations of narration are subject to the specific exigencies of the linguistic substances through which they are expressed, and an *immanent* level, constituting a sort of common structural trunk, at which narrativity is situated and organised prior to its manifestations. A common semiotic level is thus distinct from the linguistic level and is logically prior to it, whatever the language chosen for manifestation. — Greimas, 1983: 7

He has reversed the two terms we are concerned with. The *apparent level* of narration is what is constructed by the text, is what is meant by *sjuzhet/discours/discourse*, while the *immanent level* is what is meant by *fabula/histoire/story*. In other words, the narrative theory focuses on the way the literary language develops a system for the narrative content in the process of writing. Shlomith Rimmon-Kenan believes that "being an abstraction, a construct, the story is not directly available to the reader." Rather, the story is extracted from the world and is put into a narrative form for the reader to understand. But, at the same time, the story is not a "raw, undifferentiated material," but it has "its structured character, its being made of separable components, and hence having potential of forming networks of relations" (Rimmon-Kenan, 1983:6). According to Claude Bremond,

> It is the words one reads, it is the images one sees, it is gestures one deciphers, but through them it is a story one follows; and it may be the same story.
>
> — quoted in Rimmon-Kenan, 1983: 7

In the Indian fables we find that the narrative text does encapsulate the narrated event in its pristine form and develops it into a system. As put forth in the Western narrative theory, in the Indian fables the reading of the narrative text leads to an understanding of the core experience that is utilised, rearranged, and narrated that gives the story its final form. We may illustrate this concept by taking up a fable for discussion. The *Vānarinda Jātaka* (No. 57) is a famous fable originally from the Jātakas, but later adopted by the *Pañcatantra,* in which it attained more fame. This narrative is very commonly known as that of the Monkey and the Crocodile, the Monkey's heart and the wish of the Crocodile's wife to devour it.

The *fabula/histoire/story* of the fable-narrative is that there lives a monkey on a tree on the bank of a river, a crocodile lives in the same river with his wife, the two become friends, the crocodile's wife insists on eating the monkey's heart, she prevails upon her husband, the crocodile lays a trap for the monkey, and the latter outwits him. This is the core story/ event. The fable-narrative develops this into a narrative text, and this process of transformation of the core story into narrative text is what the primary interest of the contemporary narrative theory is. The core story (*fabula/histoire*) is transformed into the text by the use of narrative devices. It is interesting to note how the same core story is transformed differently in the Jātaka fable and the *Pañcatantra* fable. There are major differences in the way both these compositions develop a similar core story into a narrative system.

In the Jātaka narrative, the Monkey is none other than *bodhisattva* himself. Therefore, it is but obvious that he would represent some Buddhist virtue in this narrative. The inherent requirement of this tale here is the presentation of that quality of the *bodhisattva* that is to be seen in the Monkey, and hence that determines the way the narrative text is to be arranged. Let's see how differently the Jātaka narrative and the *Pañcatantra* narrative open. The narrator in the Jātaka starts the narrative in this way,

> Once upon a time, when Brahmadatta was reigning in Benares, the *bodhisattva* came to life again as a monkey. When full-grown, he was as big as a mare's foal and enormously strong. He lived alone on the banks of the river, in the middle of which was an island. . . . — *The Jātaka*, 1990: 142

whereas the *Pañcatantra* fable starts in this fashion:

> There was a jambolin (rose-apple) tree on the shores of a sea. It was home to Raktamukha Monkey. Once an alligator Karalalmukha arrived there. Raktmukha said: "You are our guest so savour these nectar-like jambolin."
>
> — *The Pañcatantra*, 2006

As we can see, the narrative text opens differently in both cases, preparing for the different meanings they want to signify. As the Jātaka fable is about the Buddhist discourse centred on the figure of the *bodhisattva*, the narrative twists the core story and begins by giving a befitting introduction to the liveliness of the would-be-Buddha. One interesting thing to note is that whereas in the *Pañcatantra*, the narrative text reconstructs the core event of the fable by establishing a friendship between the two, the readers find that the Monkey in the Jātaka fable does not know the Crocodile at all. In fact, from the time the Monkey sees the Crocodile, in his deceptive form, he thinks about the way to outwit him. There is no previous friendship between the two which is constructed in the *Pañcatantra* fable. The first time when the Monkey sees the Crocodile in the Jātakas, it is with apprehension:

> So when he saw that, though the water stood at the same level, the rock seemed to stand higher out of the river, he

> suspected that a crocodile might be lurking there to catch him. And in order to find out the facts of the case, he shouted, as though addressing the rock. . . . — *The Jātaka*, 1990: 142

The difference in the structure of these two texts, based on a single core story, suggests that the narrative system they seek to develop is in terms of something beyond the core story. In the Jātaka fable, as unlike the *Pañcatantra* fable, the narrative is arranged in terms of the Buddhist discourse.

There are other interesting developments in the narrative text of each fable. As pointed out we are able to suggest clearly the distinction between the two fundamental levels of narrative, as enumerated by the theorists of narrative, because we have the same *fabula/histoire/story* to deal with. In the *Pañcatantra* fable, the narrative text develops a very close friendship between the Crocodile and the Monkey. Their friendship is so close that the Crocodile's wife has to threaten her husband with suicide for convincing him to get the heart of the Monkey. Again the Crocodile's wife wants to eat the heart of the Monkey, because she thinks that after having eaten those jambolins he must be having a sweet heart, while there is no such context in the Jātaka fable. In the Jātaka fable, the Crocodile easily agrees to his wife's demand, as there is no friendship between the two.

Further, while the Monkey has a discussion with the Crocodile, in the *Pañcatantra,* about his having left his heart on the tree on the bank of the river, there is no such conversation in the Jātaka narrative, where we come across a statement spoken directly by the narrator to the reader:

> Now you must know that when crocodiles open their mouths, their eyes shut. So, when this crocodile unsuspiciously opened his mouth, his eyes shut. And there he waited with closed eyes and open jaws! Seeing this, the

> wile monkey made a jump on to the crocodile's head, and thence, with a spring, like lightning, gained the bank.

The two fables construct their narrative units differently because they are committed to expressing different discourses. The narrative in the Jātaka fable is subject to the following message, as uttered by the Crocodile:

> Whoso, O monkey-king, like you, combines
> Truth, foresight, fixed resolves, and fearlessness,
> Shall see his routed foeman turn and flee.
>
> — *The Jātaka*, 1990: 143

Whereas, the pointed moral of the narrative that influences the construction of the fable in the *Pañcatantra*, is that

> One not worthy of trust should not be trusted and even trustworthy cannot be trusted too much. The very fear arising out of trusting another can uproot you and destroy you totally. — *The Pañcatantra*, 2006: 478

Thus, these two different discourses are at the centre of the two fables, and, so, the narrative units of the core story are combined differently into the narrative systems of the two fables. One unique aspect of the narrative stylisation which accounts for the way the narrative text is constructed in the Jātakas is the alternative presence of the mediated and unmediated narration.

As pointed out above, the narrative is either directly revealed to the reader or, on occasions, there intrudes the narrator with discourse markers such as, "For the story goes that . . ." or, "Now you must know that. . . ." These discourse markers and the narrator's perspective that they introduce often help in constructing the narrative text. Seymour Chatman, in his essay, "The Structure of Narrative Transmission," calls such instances of direct narration and the intrusion of the narrator's voice as two distinct kinds of narrative presentation:

> . . . kinds of narrative presentation which includes as its two subclasses *showing* and *telling* (always remembering that *narrative* showing is different from, say, theatrical showing). We can distinguish two broad categories, according to whether or not there is an explicit narrator, and if there is, whether his existence is obvious, that is overt, or covert. — Chatman, 2004: 98

Indeed, it is the presence of the explicit narrator that influences the way the text is constructed. The explicit narrator performs two functions in the Jātaka fable: first, that of validating the supreme quality of the *bodhisattva* by making statements outside the purview of the core story; and second, co-opting the reader in the telling of the narrative.

Conclusion

THE fable has been a preferred narrative genre in India. The avowed aim of this study has been to foreground the fable-compositions in the sense of a tradition, while maintaining the inherent distinctiveness of each composition. The analysis of the various texts of this tradition makes it possible to make a few observations about them and also suggest the course further study on the subject could take. While some of the ideas that emanate from the study of these fables equally apply to the various texts of other narrative genres in India, some thoughts are specific to the fables.

Issues like the narrative and its discursive function, narrative as independent of the author, and philosophy as the basis of narrative relate as much to the fables as to any non-fable narrative in India. But there are certain specific points about the Indian fable. The discursive function of the fable is much more precisely focused than in any other narrative; each fable develops its own philosophical/political/ethical system; there is a greater sense of form about the fable than the non-fable-narratives like the fairy tale; the narrativity of the fable is a much more conscious act and the relationship between narrative and discourse is well worked out here as also the relationship between the prose and the poetic forms.

The idea underlying the fable is not to tell a story, or to depict a character, or a situation, but to depict a character or situation in order to make a point more forceful than if otherwise stated. There is an understanding that Indian people knew the viability of the fable-form, the very idea of employing the fable as a part of the situation. Bhīṣma is lying down on the bed of arrows, slowly but surely he is marching towards death. He is entreated by the Pāṇḍavas to impart them valuable knowledge on polity and ethics. Every narrative is a concentrated act, which is no fiction, not other-worldly, but, conversely, every aspect of the fable relates to the human world. The narrative is the most symbolic act here. From the moment Bhīṣma starts, for example, the fable of the Jackal and the Tiger, the listener knows that a point is going to be proved. And, hence at every stage the narrative enacts a part of that final discursive thought. This is the reason why the fable as a discourse is much more concentrated than the other non-fable narratives.

Each fable has an immediate objective. The *Pañcatantra* is addressed to princes who are extremely averse to learning; the Jātakas too address the masses. In the Jātakas, in fact, the narrative is very closely linked to the problems that inspire the telling of the narrative. Therefore, the listeners even know as does the narrator that the narrative is exclusively devoted to a particular religious discourse. The fable does not tell things to be done or aimed at, but the fables become those things, through the actions of the characters. This is how a discourse co-opts a fable completely.

The fables delineate tradition, because, as discussed they grew as a different type of literature. The sharing of the stories and story-motifs has also been phenomenal in this tradition. There have been enormous intertextual associations among all the fable-compositions, and yet it is remarkable how each composition posits its own specific agenda. Each composition represents a specific stream of the fable-tradition. The *Pañcatantra,* in particular, with its numerous recensions throughout the world reveals how sweeping in its influence a text can become. From its own adaptations of the Jātaka fables to itself being adapted in the folk narratives around the world, the text puts forth significant points about textuality.

Indeed, the relationship of the fables with the folk culture comes in a way more expressed in the fables than the non-fable narratives. The thing to remember is that a fable, like in the *Pañcatantra*, can both be placed in the academic context as well as the folk context. With numerous allusions to the *Arthaśāstra, Nāṭyaśāstra, Nītiśāstra,* and the like it would seem as if the fable would be frozen in the academic circles, but the fact that such texts later became an integral part of the folk imagination goes on to show that even the authoritative texts of the Indian culture, because they were the part of the oral tradition, disseminated well in the social sphere, so that allusions to them in the fable enhanced their interests. Likewise, though the Jātakas must have been known primarily as religious discourses, they became so absorbed in the folk that eventually led to the famous inscriptions on the *stūpa*s.

Indeed, the fables of India contain a great treasure-house of knowledge, and shed significant lights on the ancient Indian history, while their inventiveness of form, and their aesthetics, make them stories of all times. The Indian fables are both temporal and timeless.

Bibliography

Primary Sources

Aryaśur, *Jātakamālā* (*Garland of Buddha's Birth Stories*), Critically ed. Hendrik Kern, Leiden 1890 (reprint: Indological Book House, Varanasi, 1972).

Bhāgavata Purāṇa

The Hitopadeśa or The Book of Good Counsel, tr. into English by B. Hale-Wortham London: George Routledge and Sons Ltd., 1924.

The Jātaka or Stories of the Buddha's Former Births, tr. from the Pāli by Various hands under the Editorship of E.B. Cowell, Delhi: Motilal Banarsidass, 1990.

The Mahābhārata, tr. into English by M.N. Dutt, Delhi: Parimal Publications, 1997.

The Mahābhārata, tr. into English by J.A.B. Van Buitenen, London: University of Chicago Press, 1973.

The Mahābhārata, tr. into English by Kisari Mohan Ganguli, New Delhi: Munshiram Manoharlal, 1990-92.

The Pañcatantra, tr. into English by Vijay Narain, Delhi: Chaukhamba Sanskrit Pratishthan, 2006.

The Pañcatantra, tr. into English by Chandra Rajan, London: Penguin Books, 1993.

Yogavāsiṣṭha of Vālmīki, tr. into English by Viharilal Mitra, with an Introduction by Ravi Prakash Arya, Delhi: Parimal Publications, 1998.

Secondary Sources

Altekar, A.S., *Education in Ancient India*, Aligarh: Nand Kishore Brothers, 1957.

Bakhtin, Mikhail, "Discourse in the Novel", in Bran Nicol (ed.), *Postmodernism and the Contemporary Novel: A Reader*, Edinburgh: Edinburgh University Press, 2002.

———, "Discourse Typology in Prose", tr. by Richard Balthazar and I.R. Titunik, in Vassilis Lambropoulos and David Neal Miller (eds.), *Twentieth Century Literary Theory*, New York: State University of New York Press, 1987.

Balasubrahmanyam, "Introduction", The *Hitopadeśa*, 1989: 17.

Barthakuria, Chandra Apurba, *India in the Age of the Pañcatantra*, Calcutta: Punthi-Pustak, 1992.

Barthes, Roland, "Introduction to the Structural Analysis of Narratives", in Stephen Heath (ed.), *Image-Music-Text*, London: Fontana, 1977.

———, "From Work to Text", in Stephen Heath (ed.), *Image-Music-Text*, London: Fontana, 1977.

Belvalkar, S.K. (tr.), *Kāvyādarśa of Daṇḍin*, Poona: The Oriental Book Agency, 1924.

Bhattacharya, Bishnupada, *A Study in Language and Meaning*, Calcutta: Progressive Publishers, 1962.

Blackham, Stuart H. and A.K. Ramanujan (eds.), *Another Harmony: New Essays in the Folklore of India*, Delhi: Oxford University Press, 1986.

Blackham, H.J., *The Fable as Literature*, London: The Athlone Press, 1985.

Brockhaus, *Panchtantra: Fünf Bücher indischer Fablen, Märchen und Erzählungen*, Leipzig, 1859.

Brown, W.N., *The Pañcatantra in Modern Indian Folklore*, New Haven: Yale University Press, 1919.

Chaitanya, Krishna, *Sanskrit Poetics*, Bombay: Asia Publishing House, 1965.

Chatman, Seymour, *Story and Discourse: Narrative Structure in Fiction and Film*, Ithaca: Cornell University Press, 1978.

———, "The Structure of Narrative Transmission", in Julie Rivkin and Michael Ryan (eds.), *Literary Theory: An Anthology*, Oxford: Blackwell Publishing, 2004.

Coomaraswamy, Anand K. and Sister Nivedita, *Myths of the Hindu and Buddhists*, New York: Dover Publications Inc., 1967.

Crites, Stephen, "The Narrative Quality of Experience", in Stanley Hauerwas and L. Gregory Jones (eds.), *Why Narrative? Readings in Narrative Theology*, Michigan: W.B. Berdmans, 1989.

Crooke, William, *The Popular Religion and Folklore of Northern India*, 2 vols., Allahabad: Government Press, 1894, rpt., New Delhi: Munshiram Manoharlal, 1978.

Dasgupta, S.N., *A History of Indian Philosophy*, 5 vols., Delhi: Motilal Banarsidass, 2000.

De, S.K., *History of Sanskrit Poetics*, 2nd edn., 2 vols., Calcutta: K.L Mukhopadhyaya, 1960.

Deussen, Paul, *Philosophy of the Upanishads*, Edinburgh: Edinburgh: University Press, 1965.

Dhayagude, Suresh, *Western and Indian Poetics: A Comparative Study*, Pune: Bhandarkar Oriental Research Institute, 1981.

Dorson, Richard, *The British Folklorists: A History*, Chicago: University of Chicago Press, 1968.

Dwivedi, R.C. (ed.), *Principles of Literary Criticism in Sanskrit*, Delhi: Motilal Banarsidass, 1969.

Dwivedi, R.C. (tr.), *Kāvyaprakāśa of Mammaṭa*, Delhi: Motilal Banarsidass, 1966.

Foucault, Michel, *The Order of Things*, New York: Vintage Books, 1984.

———, "What is an Author", in Robert Con Davis and Ronald Schleifer (eds.), *Contemporary Literary Criticism: Literary and Cultural Studies*, New York and London: Longman, 1989.

Genette, Gerard, *Narrative Discourse*, Lewin and Culler (tr.), UK: Basil Blackwell and Oxford, 1980.

Gerow, Edwin. *A Glossary of Indian Figures of Speech*, Mounton: The Haque, 1971.

Ghosh, Manmohan (tr.), *Nāṭyaśāstra of Bharatamuni*, Calcutta: Asiatic Society, 1950.

Greimas, A.J. and H.S. Gill, *Structural Semantics*, New Delhi: Bahri Publications, 1989.

Heimann, Betty, *Indian and Western Philosophy*, London: George Allen and Unwin, 1977.

Hertel, *Panchtantra*: Harvard Oriental Series, vol. 14, 1908: 143.

Hiriyanna, M., *Outlines of Indian Philosophy*, London: Thames and Hudson, 1968.

Hopkins, Washburn E., *The Great Epic of India: Character and Origin of the Mahabharata*, Delhi: Motilal Banarsidass, 1993.

Islam, Mazharul, *A History of Folktale Collections in India and Pakistan*, Dacca: Bengali Academy, 1970.

Iyengar, K.R. Srinivasa, "The *Mahabharata:* An Epic of Universality and Deep Human Concern", in R.N. Dandekar, *The Mahabharata Revisited*, Delhi: Sahitya Akademi, 1990.

Jacques Derrida, "Psyche: Inventions of the Other", republished in D. Attridge, ed., *Acts of Literature*, 1992.

Jameson, Frederic, *The Political Unconscious: Narrative as a Socially Symbolic Art*, Ithaca: Cornell University Press, 1981.

Johnson-Davies, Denys, *Animal Tales of the Arab World*, Cairo: Hoopoe Books, 1995.

Kane, P.V., *History of Sanskrit Poetics*, 4th edn., Delhi: Motilal Banarsidass, 1971.

Kantak, V.Y., *Perspectives on Indian Literary Culture*, Delhi: Pencraft International, 1996.

Kapoor, Kapil, *Literary Theory: Indian Conceptual Framework*, New Delhi: Affiliated East-West Press Pvt. Ltd., 1998.

Kawthekar, P.N., "Fables in the Mahabharata", in *Felicitation Volume: A Collection of Forty-Five Indological Essays*, Nagpur: Vidarbha Samshodhan Mandal, 1965.

Krishnamoorthy, K. (tr.), *Dhvanyāloka of Ānandavardhana*, Delhi: Motilal Banarsidass, 1982.

——— (tr.), *Vakroktijīvitam of Kuntaka*, Dharwad: Karnataka University, 1977.

Krishnamoorthy, K., *Some Thoughts on Indian Aesthetics and Literary Criticism*, Mysore: University of Mysore, 1968.

———, *Studies in Indian Aesthetics and Criticism*, Mysore: D.V.K. Moorthy, 1979.

———, *Indian Literary Theories*, New Delhi: Meharchand Lachhmandas, 1985.

Kristeva, Julia, *Desire in Language: A Semiotic Approach to Literature and Art*, Oxford: Basil Blackwell, 1984.

Kunjani Raja, K., *Indian Theories of Meaning*, Madras: Adyar Library, 1963.

Kuppuswami Sastri, M., *Highways and Byways of Literary Criticism in Sanskrit*, Madras: The Kuppuswami Sastri Research Institute, 1945.

Kushwaha, M.S., *New Perspectives on Indian Poetics*, Lucknow: Agro Publishing House, 1991.

——— (ed.), *Indian Poetics and Western Thought*, Lucknow: Agro Publishing House, 1988.

Lahiri, P.C., *Concept of Rīti-Guṇa in Sanskrit Poetics* (rpt.), Delhi: V.K. Publishing House, 1987.

Lévi-Strauss, Claude, *Structural Anthropology* (tr.), Claire Jacobson and Brooke Grundfest Schoepf, New York: Basic Books, 1963.

———, *The Raw and the Cooked*, John and Dorean Wightman (tr.). New York: Harper and Row, 1969.

Lyotard, Jean Francois, *The Postmodern Condition*, Geoff Bennington and Brian Massumi (tr.), Minneapolis: University of Minnesota, 1982.

Martin, Wallace, *Recent Theories of Narrative*, Ithaca: Cornell University Press, 1986.

Mukherjee, B.N., *The Genesis of Buddhism: Its Social Content*, Calcutta: Pilgrim Publisher, 1976.

Pandey, K.C., *Indian Aesthetics* (vol. 1 of Comparative Aesthetics), 2nd edn. Varanasi: Chowkhamba Sanskrit Series, 1959.

Panikkar, Raimundo, *The Vedic Experience: Mantramanjari*, London: Darton, Longman and Todd, 1977, rpt. edn., Delhi: Motilal Banarsidass, 2001.

Panikker, K. Ayyappa, *Indian Narratology*, New Delhi: IGNCA and Sterling Publishers, 2003.

Pathak, R.S. (ed.), *Indian Response to Literary Theories*, Delhi: Creative Books, 2 vols., 1996.

Pathak, Suniti Kumar, *The Indian Nitisastras in Tibet*, Delhi: Motilal Banarsidass, 1974.

Pawate, C.I., *The Pañcatantra and Aesop's Fables: A Study in Genre*, Delhi: Amar Prakashan, 1986.

Penzer, N.M. (ed.), *The Ocean of Story*, 10 vols. (rpt.), Delhi: Motilal Banarsidass, 1968.

Radhakrishnan, S. (ed.), *Sourcebook of Indian Philosophy*, London: George Allen and Unwin, 1964.

———, *The Principal Upanishads*, London: George Allen and Unwin, 1953.

Raghavan, V. (tr.), *Śṛṅgāraprakāśa of Bhoja*, Madras: Punarvasu, 1963.

Raghavan and Nagendra (eds.), *An Introduction to Indian Poetics*, Delhi: Macmillan India, 1970.

———, *Studies on the Concept of Alaṁkāra Śāstra*, Madras: Adyar Library, 1973.

Ramanujan, A.K., *Folktales from India: A Selection of Oral Tales from Twenty-two Languages*, New York: Pantheon Book, 1971.

Rayan, Krishna, *Text and Sub-Text*, London and New Delhi: Arnold Heimemann, 1987.

———, *The Burning Bush: Suggestion in Indian Literature*, New Delhi: B.R. Publishers, 1988.

———, *Sahitya: A Theory of Indian Critical Practice*, New Delhi: Sterling Publishers, 1991.

Redfield, Robert, *The Little Community: Viewpoints for the Study of Human Whole*, Chicago: University of Chicago Press, 1957.

Ricoeur, Paul, *Time and Narrative*, 3 vols., Kathleen McLaughlin and David Pellauer (tr.), Chicago: University of Chicago Press, 1984.

Rimmon-Kenan, Shlomith, *Narrative Fiction: Contemporary Poetics*, London and New York: Methuen, 1983.

Sastri, Gaurinath, *The Philosophy of Word and Meaning*, Calcutta: Sanskrit College Research Series, 1959.

Sastri, P.V. Nagnath (tr.), *Kāvyālaṁkāra of Bhāmaha*, Delhi: Motilal Banarsidass, 1977.

Sharma, A. (ed.), *Essays in the Mahābhārata*, Leiden: Brill, 1991.

Sharma, S.N., *Buddhist Social and Moral Education*, Delhi: Parimal Publications, 1994.

Smith, J.D., *Tradition of Heroic and Epic Poetry*, London: Modern Humanities Research Association, 1980.

Sontag, Susan (ed.), *A Barthes Reader*, New York: Hill and Wang, 1982.

Temple, R.C., *Legends of Panjab* (rpt.), Patiala: Punjabi University, Department of Languages, 1963.

Verma, Prativa, *Social Philosophy of the Mahābhārata and the Manusmṛti*, New Delhi: Classical Publishing Company, 1988.

Vijayavardhana, G., *Outlines of Sanskrit Poetics*, Varanasi: Chowkhamba Sanskrit Series, 1970.

Wadley, Susan, *Texts in Contexts: Oral Traditions and the Study of Religion*, New Delhi: Manohar, 1978.

Warder, A.K., *Indian Kavya Literature*, Delhi: Motilal Banarsidass, 1974.

———, *The Science of Criticism in India*, Madras: Adyar Library and Research Center, 1978.

Watts, Alan W., *Myth and Ritual in Christianity*, London: Methuen, 1953.

Winternitz, Maurice, *A History of Indian Literature*, tr. from the German by Subhadra Jha, Delhi: Motilal Banarsidass, 1977.

Wood, Ramsay, *Kalila and Dimna, Selected Fables of Bidpai* (with an Introduction by Doris Lessing), Illustrated by Margaret Kilrenny, New York: Alfred A. Knopf 1980.

———, *Kalila and Dimna, Tales for Kings and Commoners, Selected Fables of Bidpai* (with an Introduction by Doris Lessing), Vermont, USA: Inner Traditions International, 1986.

———, *Kalila und Dimna, oder die Kunst, Fruende zu gewinnen, Fabeln des Bidpai*, (Vorwort von Doris Lessing), Freiberg: Herder/Spektrum, 1996.

Wortham, "Preface", The *Hitopadeśa*, 1924: vi-vii.

Web Sources

The Rig Veda: http://www.sacred-texts.com/hin/rigveda/

The Upanishads: http://www.gutenberg.org/ebooks/3283.

Mahabharata, tr. Kisari Mohan Ganguli: http://www.mahabharataonline.com/translation/index.php

Mahabharata retold by C. Rajagopalachari. Compiled and Edited by Jay Mazo, International Gita Society: http://home.att.net/~gitaprasad/mahabharata.htm

Jatakamala http://www.borobudur.tv/jataka_030.htm

Banerjee, Radha, *Pali Literature*: http://www.ibiblio.org/radha/rdindex1.htm

Blackburn, Stuart "The Brahmin and the Mongoose: The Narrative Context of a Well-Traveled Tale", in *Bulletin of the Oriental and African Studies*, University of London, vol. 59, no. 3 (1996): http://www.jstor.org/

De, Sushil Kumar, "The *Akhyayika* and the *Katha* in Classical Sanskrit", in *Bulletin of the School of Oriental Studies*, University of London, vol. 3, no. 3, 1924: http://www.jstor.org/

Edgerton, Franklin, "The Hindu Beast Fable in the Light of Recent Studies", in *The American Journal of Philology*, vol. 36, no. 1 (1915): http://www.jstor.org/

Ingalls, Daniel H.H., "The Chanakya Collections and Narayana's *Hitopadesha*", in *Journal of the American Oriental Society*, vol. 86, no.1 (January-March 1966): http://www.jstor.org/

Jacobs, Joseph, *Indian Fairy Tales*: http://www.sacred-texts.com/hin/ift/ift01.htm

Jackson, A.V. Williams, "Jataka Tales", in *The Journal of American Folklore*, vol. 31, no. 120 (April-June 1918): http://www.jstor.org/

Roy, Kum Kum, "Justice in the *Jatakas*", in *Social Scientist*, vol. 24, no. 4/6, (April-June 1996): http://www.jstor.org/

Sternbach, Ludwik, "Hitopadesha and its Sources", in *American Oriental Series*, vol. 44: http://www.jstor.org/

———, "Chanakya's Aphorisms in the Hitopadesha", in *Journal of the American Oriental Society*, vol. 76, no. 2 (April-June 1956): http://www.jstor.org/

———, *Chanakya-Niti: Text Tradition*, Hoshiarpur: Visveshwaranand Vedic Research Institute, 1963-64: http://www.jstor.org/

Index